The amazing story of...

Jesus in the
Great Escape

Out of Egypt I have
called my Son

Exodus

4

The amazing story of . . .

Jesus in the Great Escape

Out of Egypt I have called my Son

Exodus

[Moses] . . . led them out, having worked wonders and signs in Egypt, in the Red Sea, and in the wilderness for forty years. This is that Moses, who said to the children of Israel, 'The Lord our God will raise up a *prophet-like-me* for you from among your brothers . . . ' **Acts 7:36–37**

Because Jesus is the salvation that Moses modelled!

Published by PUSH Publishing 2019

www.pushpublishing.co.uk

in partnership with Jesus Centred Bible

office@jesuscentred.org

www.jesuscentred.org

Scripture quotations are based on the World English Bible (WEB) which is in the public domain. The WEB is a 1997 revision of the American Standard Version of 1901.

A catalogue record for this book is available from the British Library

ISBN-13: 978-1-912947003

Printed and bound in Great Britain by Cambrian Printers

Cover design by Joseph Laycock

Contents

Dedication

Special thanks to:

Ann Handford whose tireless support and organisation has helped me to get this material out of my head, first onto PowerPoint and teaching notes, then into manuals and books.

And to the family of partners who believe in this series of books and make them happen by their support. I want to mention the following here:

Jason Fisher, John Hicklin, David Jacklin, Paul and Anne Lloyd, Nigel and Wendy Preston, John and Gill Sandeman, Ruth Senior, Diane Sinclair, Richard and Bozy Spencer, Di Steele and Jon Walker.

Thank you!

Introduction

J oseph took Mary and newborn Jesus to Egypt to escape Herod, **Matthew 2:13**. **Origen** tells us they were there for two years before returning to Nazareth. And so, 'what was spoken by the Lord through the prophet, saying, "Out of Egypt I called my son" . . . ' happened all over again, **Matthew 2:15** quoting **Hosea 11:1**.

This is a very Hebrew way of understanding prophecy and history. *YHWH*'s 'Word' was living and it produced fruit, not just once but time and again. So, the Gospels present events in Jesus' life as the re-workings of Israel's prophetic story. As the incarnate 'Word', Jesus embodied everything that *YHWH* had previously communicated. The thing that unified all prophecy, whether written as text or acted out in history, was its testimony to Jesus, **Revelation 19:10**.

Now, John starts his Gospel like the book of **Genesis**, 'In the beginning . . . ', but his prologue concludes:

> . . . and The Word became flesh, and lived in a tent (tabernacled) among us. We saw his glory, glory like the only-born of the Father, full of grace and truth. **John 1:14**

. . . which is a reference to the final verse of **Exodus**:

> For the cloud of *YHWH* was on the tabernacle by day, and there was fire in the cloud by night throughout all their journeys. **Exodus 40:38**

. . . because **Exodus** provides the great historical archetype of 'salvation' (ישוע) for which Jesus / Salvation / ישוע is the anti-type. *The Great Escape* was a story, simple enough to be told to children but with deeper meaning for those who cared to look, **Psalm 78:2,6,12+**. *The Great Escape* is a parable of the Gospel:

- In both: God's people are governed by a foreign power when a saviour is born.

- In both: The infant saviour survives an attempt on his life by a bad king.

- The inaugural Passover happens in **Exodus**, the ultimate Passover happens in the Gospels.

- In both: Fifty days after Passover, a Covenant is ratified with a gift . . .

  - In the Old Covenant, the Law is given and 3000 die for their sins.

  - In the New, the Spirit is given and 3000 people receive new life.

Exodus is to the Old Testament, what the Gospels are to the New Testament.

The Great Escape was a message written in the ink of history. As history, the events of **Exodus** are so redolent with truth that, like the Gospel, their story becomes a myth. Not in the sense of being untrue, but in the sense that something of Heaven is present in the telling of these earthly events. The Gospel and the *Exodus* are so effective as myths that there are devout Christians and Jews who doubt their history whilst building their lives on the meaning of them. But there should be no conflict. As **CS Lewis** observed:

> . . . the story of Christ is simply a *true* myth: a myth working on us in the same way as the others [pagan myths], but with this tremendous difference *that it really happened*.

> Undeceptions, 1971

As we look for Jesus in *the Exodus* we don't want to get bogged down in historical theories, but neither do we want to ignore them. Our expectations of God are profoundly changed if we see Him not just as the author of a great story, but as an artist working in the lives, actions and experiences of real people living through extraordinary events. As an artist, *YHWH* doesn't just paint a picture to be admired, He illuminates an invitation to participation, one that requires a response.

So we will tell the story of **Exodus**, affirming and illustrating it with the facts of archaeology and secular history, while at the same time drawing out its theology and revelation of salvation / Jesus.

In *Volume 1: Jesus in the Old Testament* we saw that *YHWH* speaks in both parables and knotty puzzles that need to be untangled. And so, we will find Jesus in both the big picture and hidden in the text of **Exodus**, in the mystery and in the history.

Using these notes

The table on page 5 lists all seven streams of revelation used in this series to show how Jesus is presented in the Old Testament. Each stream appears in the book of **Exodus**, but the 'salvation' metaphor makes Typology (📖) its major revelation, often Teaching (📖) us something theological too.

This book is arranged into four *Sections*.

> *Section 1*: Context and Consequence
>
> *Section 2*: Moses . . . Hebrews in Egypt, birth, growing up, Midian
>
> *Section 3*: Plagues and Passover
>
> *Section 4*: The Exodus and The Road to Sinai

Please note, **Strong's** numbers are often given to aid further research, in the form #HXXXX for Hebrew words and #GXXXX for Greek.

So, let's get started!

Prophecy: Predictive, Ecstatic and Formative

 Typology: Models, Titles, People and Events

 Teaching: Used by or about Jesus / Gospels

 Jesus' Household: The Family Tree

 Trinity and Divinity: Jesus as God /
God as a Plurality

 Christophanies: God in visible form

 Cryptic: Hidden in the Hebrew

Part 1

Context & Consequence

Questions and Connections

When I was eleven, my school spent a term looking at Biblical events as secular history. It was fascinating to discover that Jericho's walls really had collapsed just as we read in the book of **Joshua**.

Now, scholarship of the time believed that Jericho had been overrun well before Joshua arrived on the scene, but my history teacher was wise enough to know the difference between facts and opinions. It is a fact that at some point Jericho's walls collapsed but it is a 'considered opinion' that the date was too early for the Bible's account. Unfortunately, opinions, once formed, are often hard to displace.

So, I grew up reading archaeological opinion that was sure that King David never existed and that *the Exodus* didn't happen. But in 1993 a stone fact forced critics to change their opinion on David. A victory stele dating from the ninth century BC was excavated in Tel Dan. It refers unequivocally to the 'house of David' confirming an earlier damaged, but disputed, reference to David written on the important 'Moabite Stone'.

Today you will still read articles by 'Biblical minimalists' who 'know' that *the Exodus* didn't happen and that there is 'no evidence' for it, but they are a fading voice. With every new excavation, and with the computer cataloguing of vast amounts of older findings and facts, our understanding and the secular likelihood of some sort of historical *Exodus* grows.

This book is about how Jesus is revealed in this *Exodus*, so it would be easy to ignore the history and focus on meaning only. But to do so would lessen the parable's power because the experiences of *the Exodus* are what gave birth to Monotheism as a **corporate** faith. If the story didn't happen it is hard to explain why its solemn retelling is the pumping heart of Biblical and modern Judaism.

So, this book will tell the story, linking **Exodus**' revelation of Jesus on a time and story line which makes sense of current archaeological evidence. There are different ways this can be done. My aim is to foster confidence in the history of **Exodus**, not to promote a theory, so you can thread the unearthed facts onto another timeline if you would prefer.

Now, to set the historical context of *the Great Escape,* there are a couple of questions to consider before we begin . . .

Question 1: What date does the Bible give for the Exodus?

Work on Solomon's temple started 480 years after *the Exodus*.

> In the four hundred and eightieth year after the Israelites left Egypt, in the fourth year of Solomon's reign . . . He began building *YHWH*'s temple. **1 Kings 6:1**

We can date Solomon's reign quite confidently because

Israel's history is closely intertwined with Assyrian history, and Assyrian dating is linked to astronomical observations which modern science can verify. Solomon's reign is usually reckoned to have started around 970 BC. Subtracting 480 years from 970 BC gives 1450 BC as a good benchmark for *the Exodus*.

But many believe *the Exodus* happened 200 years later, around 1250 BC. They assume that '480 years' is a symbolic, not literal, number. The logic goes like this:

1) 480 = 12 × 40, and the Bible often uses the numbers 12 and 40 *qualitatively* rather than *quantitatively*. The number 12 represents God's order or government, and 40 represents a generation.

2) A generation is not actually 40 years, it is around 20 to 25 so the real elapsed time is 12 generations, 240–300 years.

3) *The Exodus* happened around 240-300 years before 970 BC – circa 1250 BC.

A date of 1250 BC is part of the current **Standard** historical view of *the Exodus*. *The Exodus* is certainly possible at that time, but 1450 BC is the more straightforward way of understanding the Biblical date.

Professor Kenneth Kitchen, one of the world's leading experts on Egyptian chronology has made the point:

> There are two options . . . you've got . . . the early date (1450 BC) and you've got the late Bronze

age option (1250 BC) . . . these are two powerful sets of options which do not give credence to the mythologists (ie the Exodus deniers).

So, from the Bible, we have two possible dates for *the Exodus*, 1250 BC or 1450 BC.

Question 2: What was happening in Egypt at that time?

This is not an easy question to answer because, while there is a standard timeline for Egyptian History, it has been called 'a rubber chronology' (**Professor Heinrich Otten**) because it must be stretched and squashed to accommodate new facts and other ancient histories.

Fitting this timeline to *the Exodus* depends on how we link Egyptian and Biblical chronology together. The whole Egyptian / African timeline prior to 1000 BC is tied into the Eurasian ancient world (and consequently Assyrian, Greek and Babylonian history) by a single coincidence with the Bible – the campaign of Shishak in **1 Kings 14:25**.

The Accepted Connection

In the nineteenth century **Jean Francois Champollion**, who first deciphered Egyptian hieroglyphs, translated an inscription which described a military campaign by a Pharoah called 'Shoshenk'. It listed cities found in the Bible and even referred to the 'Kingdom of Judah'. **Champollion** assumed that this Pharoah Shoshenk was the same as the one called 'Shishak' who fought Rehoboam I in **1 Kings 14:25**.

If Shishak was Shoshenk **and** *the Exodus* happened around 1450 BC, then Thutmose II is the most likely candidate for *the Exodus* Pharoah. Accepting the later date, 1250 BC, gives us Ramesses II, Egypt's most famous king. Hollywood has helped fix Ramesses II as the presiding Pharoah in our minds as the **Standard** model of *the Exodus*.

Over the last century academics have worked hard to fit Egyptian chronology around this connection between Biblical Shishak and Egyptian Shoshenk.

An Alternative Connection

As scholarship has deepened its understanding of Egyptian texts, it has become apparent that the description of Shoshenk's campaign does not match the Biblical description of Shishak's campaign in **1 Kings**. Additionally, recent work on the development of the ancient Hebrew alphabet (see *Volume 1: Jesus in the Old Testament*) has highlighted that Ramesses II himself is a better fit for the Biblical Shishak than is Shoshenk.

It is well-attested that Ramesses II used the short name 'Sisw', pronounced 'Sisoo'. Using bronze age Hebrew pictograms this is written $\mathcal{P}$(oo)$\mathbf{w}$(s)$\mathbf{Z}$(i)$\mathbf{w}$(s) – reading right to left. By the Iron age the pictogram representing the 'oo' sound, the final letter wav-ו / $\mathcal{P}$, had changed its shape to Υ while the shape $\mathcal{P}$ now represented the letter qoph-ק, which produces the 'k' sound. So, Ramesses / *Sisw* / $\mathcal{P}\mathbf{w}\mathbf{Z}\mathbf{w}$ would eventually be read as either 'Sisak' or Shishak, the Pharaoh who fought Rehoboam I.

It is easy to imagine how a second-century Temple scribe, transferring Biblical texts onto scrolls using fifth-century Hebrew glyphs may have misread ϘwᏃw / *Sisw* as Shishak. The scribe may even have transferred it this way deliberately because 'Shishak' sounds like the Hebrew for 'entrapped gift' or an 'appeasing gift' – from *shi* / שי (#H7862) which was 'a gift (to the Temple)' and *shakak* / שכך (#H7918) meaning 'entrap' or 'appease'. And whoever Shishak was, in the Biblical account he entrapped Jerusalem and was appeased by removing the gold and silver from the Temple, **2 Chronicles 12:9**.

If Ramesses II is Shishak, it drags that rubber Egyptian chronology forward by a massive 300 years. This is too much for many to accept but resolves a lot of puzzles – such as the appearance of Biblical names like Joseph and Levi attached to Egyptian monuments and appearing in Egyptian documents years before these characters were born if we accept the **Standard** connection and a late date for *the Exodus!*

This reworked Egyptian timeline is part of the Radical model. It is referred to as the **New Chronology** and it makes Dudimose II a good fit for the *Exodus* Pharoah.

Three models of the timing of the Exodus

We now have three points on the Egyptian timeline to look for *the Exodus*, as shown in the table opposite.

Exodus Model	Exodus Date	Egyptian Chronology	Pharoah of Exodus	Comment	Major proponent
Standard	Late 1250 BC	Standard	Ramesses II		Professor Kenneth Kitchen, Liverpool University
Traditional	Early 1450 BC	Standard	Thutmose II	Following a short prosperous reign his kingdom collapses with no heir. His wife Hatshepsup succeeds him.	Alfred Edersheim, Victorian Bible scholar
Radical	Early 1450 BC	New Chronology	Dudimose II	Built on the earliest and first appearances of Hebrew people in Egypt.	David Rohl, Egyptologist (still work in progress)

In this book we will trace the story using the **Radical Model** with reference to the **Traditional** and **Standard Models**. The **Radical Model** encompasses the earliest evidence of Biblical events. If *the Exodus* actually happened later, this evidence still sets precedence and context for it. Opinions will change but facts will always need to be accounted for.

Let's start the story.

Joseph and His Brothers

> Now these are the names of the sons of Israel, who came into Egypt . . . seventy souls, and Joseph was in Egypt already. **Exodus 1:1–5**

In *Volume 3: Jesus in the Fathers* we saw how Joseph stood as a type of the ascended Christ, the world saviour unrecognised by his own family until the very end. Christ was in Joseph writing His-story in Joseph's.

Modern Bibles tell us that the Israelites were in Egypt for 430 years, **Exodus 12:40**, because they follow the later Masoretic texts of the Old Testament (transcribed circa tenth century AD). But this contradicts the New Testament; the older Septuagint Texts (third century BC); the Jewish Historian **Josephus**; and the Samaritan Pentateuch (fourth century BC), which all say that the 430 years is measured from Abraham's arrival in Canaan.

The Apostle Paul says it this way:

> Now the promises were spoken to *Abraham* and
> to his seed . . . the law . . . came *four hundred
> and thirty years after* . . . **Galatians 3:16–17**

So, we need to estimate just how long the Israelites were
in Egypt.

The Bible lists between 3 and 6 generations in Egypt for
the various families of Israel. Biblical genealogies can
sometimes skip a generation, so these records could
suggest that Joseph entered Egypt 150 to 200 years
before Moses left. **Josephus** suggests 215 years (exactly
half of the 430 years). In the **Radical Model** Joseph's
story happened around 1650 BC, which is in the reign of a
Pharaoh called Amenemhat III, and his reign experienced
events covered in **Genesis**.

Famine and Floods

Egypt had a different agricultural cycle from Canaan.
During hot periods Canaan's crops suffered while Egypt's
thrived as increased snow melt from African mountains
fed the Nile and produced a higher flood level and a better
harvest. In times of Canaanite famine people left Canaan
to buy bread from Egypt . . . just as we read in **Genesis**.

So, the annual flood level was recorded for tax purposes.
During Amenemhat III's reign, Egypt had a run of extremely
good harvests until the flood level reached a height of 6.5
metres above normal. At this level the flood waters could not

subside in time for crop planting, leading to years of famine. This looks like the disaster Joseph foresaw in **Genesis 41**.

The flood levels remained disastrously high for 12 years. But during this period a wise vizier seems to have completed a huge canal to drain excess water from the southern Nile into an inland lake, shortening the bad years (the Bible records 7!). This 'Great Canal' still works today and it has been known since ancient times as the *Baht Yussef*, 'The Waterway of Joseph'.

The Vizier

During this same period a new government department appears in Egypt's records, the *Kha en djed remelj* which means 'Department of the people's giving', perhaps reflecting Joseph's central administration of grain production and distributions. Amenemhat III appointed a new sub-Vizier called 'Ankhu, Overseer of the fields'. Eventually it seems this 'Ankhu' or someone else with the same name becomes Egypt's main Vizier.

Egyptian records are fitting the Biblical narrative quite well at this point but what is perhaps most remarkable is that the Bible tells us: 'Then Pharoah called Joseph "Zaphenath Paneah"', **Genesis 41:45**.

- 'Zaphenath' is the way Hebrew ears would have heard an Egyptian phrase which Egyptologists write as 'djedu en ef'. Ancient Egyptian words are vocalised according to the elements in the original hieroglyphs rather than the modern letters used to write them so, 'djedu en ef' is vocalised as 'zatenaph' and simply means 'who is called'. (We find this word used in lists of Hebrew slaves with Egyptian names in Egyptian papyri.)

Mixing up letter order is common when hearing a foreign word and 'zatenaph' becomes 'zaphenath'. So **Genesis** actually tells us that Joseph became known as 'Joseph who is called Pa-aneah!

- Pa-aneah. In ancient Egyptian 'Pa' is the word 'The' and 'aneah' is the vocalisation of 'Ankh' which means 'Life', the name of the Amenemhat III's vizier.

So the Bible records a name for Joseph which later scribes didn't understand, but which we can now translate! Joseph was given the same name as the vizier who coordinated grain production during a cycle of bumper then disastrous harvests in the reign of Amenemhat III.

If you prefer the **Traditional** or **Standard Models** for *the Exodus* then 'Joseph Zaphenath Pa-aneah' / 'Joseph who is called The-Life' must be a title deliberately given to him to associate him with this earlier vizier, who is referred to in Egyptian texts as pa-Aam / 'the Asiatic [Semite]'. Interestingly, some decades later, we find more than 1 in 10 Egyptian slaves are named after Ankhu the Semite, **Brooklyn Papyrus 35.1446**.

Exodus is off to a strong historical start. The facts of Amenemhat III's reign reflect events or set precedents and patterns that perfectly match Joseph's story.

Twelve and Seventy

When Jacob's twelve sons settled in Egypt the wider clan comprised about 70 people. The beginning seeds the outcome of **Exodus**, which ends with twelve consecrated pillars representing the 12 tribes and 70 anointed elders who saw *YHWH* with their own eyes, **Exodus 24:1,4,9**.

This pattern, of the 12 Patriarchs being represented by a community of 70 elders, continues through Israel's history eventually becoming the Jerusalem Sanhedrin, the 71 rulers who condemned Jesus to death.

Jesus appoints 12 apostles followed by 70 (or 72) ministers, **Luke 10:1**, reflecting the numbers of founders and witnesses that established the Old Covenant as He inaugurated the New. (Note: 70 is a symbolic number for eldership – in practice it covered between 70 and 74 people).

The New Covenant revolves around Jesus, the living Word, and the Old Covenant revolved around Torah, the written word. Something only possible due to a remarkable invention by an Israelite who lived in Egypt during the lifetime of Joseph . . .

The Written Word

At the beginning of the twentieth century, Egyptologists **Hilda and Flinders Petrie** came across some crudely scratched graffiti at Serabit El-Khadim, an Egyptian controlled mining area in the Sinai Peninsula. The graffiti used hieroglyphic symbols arranged in lines, but they made no sense until someone thought of reading the text as Hebrew rather than Egyptian.

This graffiti gave us the Protosiniatic alphabet which we often reference in this series of books (see the note on *Sisak / 𐤒𐤔𐤆𐤔* above). Its development through various forms into ancient Hebrew is better understood today as archaeology uncovers more and more examples of it, but the texts from Serabit El-Khadim are among the oldest. According to **Sir Alan Gardiner** who first translated them, they are dated from the reign of Amenemhat III, the Pharoah served by Joseph if we follow the **Radical Model**.

It seems that some genius from Jacob's family invented the world's *first* phonetic alphabet. Simple enough to be read and written by everyone, it allowed the Israelites to record their history and it gave us the Bible.

Who was this genius? Well it is worth noting that the name 'Levi' can be found in the scribbles at Serabit El-Khadim and it was the Levites who kept records and taught Israel its history. If it wasn't Levi himself, there is a certain logic to it being a member of his family.

Whoever the inventor was, the people first conceived by *YHWH*-the-Word (**Genesis 15:1,13–16**), who were entrusted with recording and preserving God's oracles, **Romans 3:2**, were gifted with an alphabet up to the task whilst living in Egypt.

Multiplication

> The children of Israel were fruitful, and increased abundantly, and multiplied, and grew exceedingly mighty; and the land was filled with them. Now there arose a new king over Egypt, who didn't know Joseph. **Exodus 1:8**

Within a generation of the death of Amenemhat III, the twelfth Egyptian dynasty had ended. Egypt entered a 'Second Intermediate Period', breaking up into smaller Kingdoms lead by local Pharaohs who claimed power by force and politics. These Pharaohs had no allegiance to Joseph's family or people.

In the south, 'Upper Egypt', we have evidence of the enslavement of non-indigenous peoples. A papyrus from the reign of a usurper mini-Pharoah of this intermediary period, Sobekhotep III, lists slaves by name. Two thirds of these names are Semitic and include the Biblical names 'Asher' and 'Dan' as well as the name 'Shiprah', the name of one of the midwives mentioned just before Moses is born, **Exodus 1:15**.

Sobekhotep III was succeeded by Neferhotep I, who can be linked to the Babylonian King list by a chain of recently discovered synchronisms. These synchronisms give Neferhotep I a date of around 1525 BC, 75 years before *the Great Escape* if we follow either the **Radical** or the **Traditional** view of *the Exodus*. This is when Moses is born.

In the second or third century BC, an Egyptian-Jew living in Alexandria, **Artapanus**, wrote a comical and fantastical account of the Jews in Egypt. **Artapanus** tells us that Moses' adoptive Egyptian mother eventually married a Pharoah from the neighbouring sub-Kingdom and he refers to this Pharaoh as 'Kenophres'. This name can be uniquely identified with Neferhotep I's younger brother, Pharoah Sobekhotep IV, who took the regnal name 'Kha-nefer-re'.

Moses would have been born under Neferhotep I's reign but for the fact that he was born in the north, in 'Lower Egypt', under a different sub-Pharoah. However, as Moses grew up, Lower and Upper Egypt were reunited by the marriage of his adoptive mother to Sobekhotep IV.

Using the **Radical Model**, we have found a good fit for Moses' history. But the story is also 'mythic' in its meaning and can be understood Christologically too.

 This is a good point to transfer some notes into your Bible

Part 2

Moses

Moses the Sign

> A man of the house of Levi went and took a daughter of Levi as his wife. The woman conceived, and bore a son. When she saw him, that he was good, she *hid* him for three months.
> Exodus 2:1–2

Moses was hidden for three months, his introduction hides something too! In **Exodus 2:2**, the word 'him' is a single letter, wav-ו, but it is given extra emphasis by the use of the definite object marker word we looked at in *Volume 1: Jesus in the Old Testament*, the little word *'AT'* made up of the first and last letters of the Hebrew alphabet, aleph-א and tav-ת. So 'him' is written אתו, but in the freshly invented pictograms of Moses' day they read 𐤒𐤕𐤏, creating a picture of a sacrifice-𐤏, a cross-𐤕 and a peg or nail-𐤒. These same three letters in a different order made up the word for the 'sign' of God's activity, *AWT* / 𐤕𐤒𐤏 (#H226), that we looked at in *Volume 2: Jesus in the Beginning*. With the benefit of hindsight we can see Jesus-fixed-to-a-cross in these letters.

The word *AWT* / 𐤕𐤒𐤏, the 'sign' of God's covenant, will appear 15 times in 14 verses in the book of **Exodus** (see **Exodus 3:12, 4:8,8,9,17,28,30, 7:3, 10:1,2, 12:13, 13:9,16, 31:13,17**). But here the same letter-glyph-picture of Jesus-fixed-to-a-cross introduces Moses as 'him' / *ATW* / 𐤒𐤕𐤏.

Now we should note that Hebrew grammar produces this picture every time it emphasises a 'him' or an 'it' as the direct object of a sentence, but in the book of **Exodus** that 'him' or 'it' is almost always a picture or 'type' of Christ. We catch the Holy Spirit's smile when we see 𐤐+𐤏 being used for: the Passover Lamb, **Exodus 12:7,11,14**; the Manna, **Exodus 16:21,24,33**; the Ark of the Covenant, **Exodus 25:11,24**; the Sacrificial Altar, **Exodus 27:2,7,8,21**; Aaron the High Priest, **Exodus 28:1**; the sin offering, **Exodus 29:36**; and other items that become models of Jesus.

Moses' introduction hides a hieroglyph that pointed to Jesus, because Moses is an arch-type of Christ.

Ⓗ Moses and Jesus

Moses was the mediator of *YHWH*'s first formal covenant, the agreement and promises, terms and conditions of partnership with God. Jesus fulfilled those terms and conditions on behalf of humanity and became 'the mediator of a better covenant . . . enacted on better promises', **Hebrews 8:6**.

Moses' Law defined and explained spiritual death, **Romans 7:5**. Jesus completed and fulfilled that Law, and then gave us the new 'Law of the Spirit of life in Christ Jesus' which has set you 'free from the law of sin and death', **Romans 8:2**.

Jesus is a lawgiver, like Moses, but He is also the fulfilment of Moses' message. We can see this pattern of being 'like' but going beyond Moses in multiple ways:

- **Divinity**: '*YHWH* said to Moses, "Behold, I have made you as God to Pharaoh . . . you shall speak what I tell you . . ."', **Exodus 7:1–2**. But Jesus was the Word that 'was God', **John 1:1**.

- The Apostolic **Priesthood**: The Greek word 'Apostle' means 'sent' and is used 7 times about Moses in the Greek / Septuagint version of **Exodus 3 & 4**. Moses was also the original Priest who consecrated Aaron, **Leviticus 8**, while Jesus is 'the Apostle and High Priest of our confession', **Hebrews 3:1**.

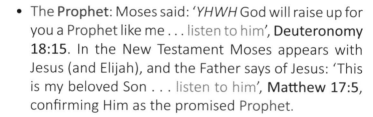

- The **Prophet**: Moses said: '*YHWH* God will raise up for you a Prophet like me . . . listen to him', **Deuteronomy 18:15**. In the New Testament Moses appears with Jesus (and Elijah), and the Father says of Jesus: 'This is my beloved Son . . . listen to him', **Matthew 17:5**, confirming Him as the promised Prophet.

- A **King**: Moses ' . . . was King in Jeshurun' (a nickname for Israel), **Deuteronomy 33:5**. 'Jesus answered, "My Kingdom is not of this world . . ."', **John 18:36**.

It is interesting to note that Moses is called 'a prophet', 'a priest' and 'a king', three roles which were recognised by anointing and which Jesus fulfilled as the Christ. However, we never read about Moses being anointed as such, instead he was recognised in each role for his actions. And so, in the covenant he mediated, holiness came by what you did, whereas in the New Covenant, holiness comes by the anointing of the Holy Spirit.

Here are 21 further parallels between Moses and Jesus:

Characterstic	Moses	Jesus
Born under Gentile rule	Egyptians	Romans
Saved from a royal death sentence	Exodus 1:15–22	Matthew 2:16–18
Rejected privileged heritage to identify with suffering people	Hebrews 11:24–25 Refused royalty for family	Philippians 2:6–7 Jesus let go of divinity for humanity
Empowered for mission by divine encounters in the wilderness	Exodus 3	Matthew 4:1–11, Mark 1:13, Luke 3:4–13
Rebuked bad Kings who wanted to kill them	Exodus 5–12 Pharaoh	Luke 13:31–32 Herod
Had to deal with the hardened hearts of others	Exodus 8:15	Mark 6:52
Healed leprosy and used the healing as a sign against unbelief	Exodus 4:6–8 Numbers 12:1–15	Matthew 8:1–4
A Shepherd	Exodus 3:1	John 10:11
Fasted for 40 days	Exodus 34:28	Luke 4:2
Brought manifesto message from a mountain	Exodus 34	Matthew 5:1

. . . continued

Humble	**Numbers 12:3**	Matthew 11:29, 21:5
Envied	**Psalm 106:16**	Matthew 27:18
Fed hungry people in a wilderness	Exodus 16	Mark 8:1–9
Water for thirsty people	Exodus 15:22–25 Water provided	John 4:10,14 Water promised
Leadership teams of 12 and then 70	Exodus 24:1–4	Luke 6:13, 10:1
Called 'My servant' by *YHWH*	**Numbers 12:7**	Matthew 12:18
A Judge	Exodus 18:13;	John 5:24–30, 8:2-5
Taught what *YHWH* had given to teach	**Deuteronomy 4:5**	John 12:49–50
Debates over body after death	Jude 1:9 Michael and the Devil	Mark 15:43–45 Joseph of Arimathea and Pilate
Death caused a divine rebuke to the Devil	Jude 1:9	Hebrews 2:14
'A son drawn out of water'	See below	See below

But we are getting ahead of ourselves . . .

The Birth of Moses

The first century Jewish historian **Josephus** adds details to the Bible's account of Moses' birth which display remarkable parallels with Jesus' nativity.

Josephus tells us that:

- An Egyptian sage had foretold an Israelite who 'would excel all men in virtue and would obtain everlasting fame' but who would be bad news for the Egyptians, just as Micah would prophecy a ruler from eternity, **Micah 5:2** (read to Herod in **Matthew 2:6**)

- This prophecy prompts Pharaoh to order the death of Hebrew boys at birth, just as prophecy would lead Herod to kill the innocents in Bethlehem, **Matthew 2:16**

- God appears to Moses' father Amram in a dream and tells him ' . . . your child. He will deliver the Hebrew nation from their bondage in Egypt, and his memory will live as long as the universe . . . ', **Josephus Antiquities II 210**, just as an Angel brings a message to Joseph from God saying Mary's son 'is of the Holy Spirit . . . He . . . will save His people . . . ', **Matthew 1:21–22**.

Josephus claims that Moses was released into the Nile as an act of faith in God's destiny. He is found by Pharaoh's daughter, Thermusis, who *imposed* this name "Mo-uses" upon him, from what happened when he was put in the river; for Egyptians call water by the name of "mou" and such as are saved out of it by "uses" . . . ' (**Antiquities II 238**).

Josephus is broadly correct in making 'uses' mean 'saved out of' but it is more generally used for a 'son' in the sense of the heir-out-of-the-family-line. So, if we fully expand the Egyptian name 'Moses' we understand it as 'a son (saved) out of water', matching what we read in the Bible: '. . . he became her son, she named him Moses saying, "Because I drew him out of the water"', **Exodus 2:10b.**

However, 'Moses' has a Hebrew meaning as well as an Egyptian one. The name sounds like the form of the verb *masha* / 'to draw out' / משא which means 'he who draws out', prophesying what Moses *will* become when he leads the people out of Egypt.

Whilst the Egyptian and Hebrew meanings of Moses' name were appropriate for Moses, they also anticipated Jesus. Jesus was declared 'My Son' as He was drawn out of the waters of the Jordan as the Beloved Son, and He became the one who draws us out of our spiritual slavery, through the waters of baptism.

Now, 'Moses' was a nickname, it was neither Moses' birthname, nor his Egyptian royal name. But interestingly, the oldest son of Sobekhotep IV (Moses' adoptive father as identified by **Artapanus**) was known as *Miu* which means 'cat' and sounds like the start of 'Mo-uses'. Cats were held in the highest esteem across Egypt but particularly in lower Egypt where Moses grew up as popular prince, **Exodus 11:3.**

Prince of Egypt

Both **Artapanus** and **Josephus** tell us that, as a young man, Moses led the Egyptian army and turned back an invasion by the Cushites (from modern-day Ethiopia). Historians didn't take this idea too seriously until in 2003 a text was uncovered in tombs at el-Kab which told about a massive Cushite invasion into Egypt during 'the Second Intermediate Period'!

According to **Josephus**, peace was achieved by a marriage alliance between Moses and Tharbis, the Princess of Ethiopia. That Moses was married as a young man will be a shock to many, but the Bible seems to refer to Tharbis: 'Miriam and Aaron spoke against Moses because of the Cushite woman whom he had married . . .', **Numbers 12:1**.

It seems that Moses was fully invested in his royal identity. He had popularity and influence with Egyptians and Ethiopians, and had not lost connection with his Hebrew family. It is easy to understand why Pharaoh tried to kill Moses after his intervention on behalf of a fellow Israelite, **Exodus 2:15**. Moses with his multicultural appeal was a risk to the emerging dynasty at a time when dynasties came and went in a generation.

So, Moses flees to Midian (South West Arabia) where he is recognised as an Egyptian not as a Hebrew, **Exodus 2:19**. Here he meets and marries Zipporah, the daughter of the local priest Reuel (also called Jethro). Moses starts a second life as a Midianite. He feels like 'a stranger in a strange land', **Exodus 2:22**, and calls his first son 'Gershom' which can either mean 'a stranger there' (ie when Moses lived in Egypt) or 'called a stranger' (ie Moses still feels like a stranger in Midian). It is into this lostness that God will act in one of history's pivotal encounters, declaring a people of faith with their own holy homeland.

Meanwhile back in Egypt Moses' step-father, the Pharaoh, dies.

The First Apostle!

YHWH appears in visible form in the burning bush, **Exodus 3 & 4**. This Theophany / Christophany is described as 'the Angel of *YHWH*' (**Exodus 3:2**) before being referred to as *YHWH* Himself (**Exodus 3:4**). However, in **Exodus 3:2** 'Angel' is the word 'Messenger' and the words 'the' and 'of' are not there in the Hebrew text, they are inferred by translators. **Exodus 3:2** reads: 'וירא מלאך יהוה' meaning (more literally) 'and Messenger *YHWH* appears'. Messenger–*YHWH* makes this Christophany a part of God, whereas '[the] Angel [of] *YHWH*' unhelpfully implies a separately created being, a cherub or seraph.

Messenger–*YHWH* is God-the-Son. The fourth-century theologian **Augustine** came to this same conclusion, writing: 'Is the Angel then the God of Abraham, the God of Isaac and the God of Jacob? Therefore he may be rightly understood to be the Saviour himself . . . ' **Augustine, On the Trinity**.

Messenger–*YHWH* commissions and sends Moses from a mountain, Jesus will commission and send people from mountains too (**Luke 6:12–16**). Both will make promises of: 'I will be with you' (**Exodus 3:12** and **Matthew 28:16,20**), and of signs following (**Exodus 3:12**, **4:8,9,17,28,30** and **Mark 16:15–18**)! And compare the words spoken to Moses, 'I will be with your mouth and teach you what you are to say', **Exodus 4:12**, with those of Jesus to His apostles, 'I will give you a mouth and wisdom which all your adversaries will not be able to counter or contradict,' **Luke 21:15** (see also **Matthew 10:19**, **Mark 13:11**, **Luke 12:11–12**). The similarities exist because Messenger–*YHWH* is the pre-incarnate Christ who became Jesus of Nazareth.

Messenger–*YHWH* uses the words 'sent' and 'send' five times to commission Moses (**Exodus 3:10,12,13,14,15**). In the ancient Greek Septuagint version of this passage, these words are all derivatives of *apostello* / ἀποστέλλω (#G649) which gives us the word 'Apostle' in the New Testament. 'Apostello' words are used twice more by Moses in this passage, **Exodus 4:13,28**, bringing the total to a spiritually indicative seven times. As a messenger, Messenger–*YHWH* is both sent and sends, He is the prime Apostle, commissioning the first Apostle. As Jesus put it, 'As the Father has sent me, even so I send you', **John 20:21**.

Resurrection and Life

 After the opening formalities, Messenger–*YHWH* declares:

 I am the God of your father, the God of Abraham, the God of Isaac and the God of Jacob. **Exodus 3:6**

Moses had married into the family of *the* Priest of Midian, **Exodus 3:1**. Midianites worshipped a moon-god but they were descended from Abraham, through his second wife Keturah, not through Sarah, **Genesis 25:1–2**. Abraham had worshipped *Elohim* who had promised a blessing through Sarah, Isaac and Jacob. God called Moses back to a neglected family with words that Jesus showed contained the Bible's first hint of the hope of resurrection and eternal life.

> On that day Sadducees (those who say that there is no resurrection) came to him [Jesus] . . . Jesus answered them, ' . . . concerning the resurrection of the dead, haven't you read that which was spoken to you by God, saying, "I am the God of Abraham, and the God of Isaac, and the God of Jacob"? God is not the God of the dead, but of the living.' **Matthew 22:23–32**, see also **Mark 12:26–27, Luke 20:37–38**

Messenger–*YHWH*'s statement to Moses implied life after death, and resurrection and life are part of the divine name '*YHWH*' about to be revealed. While '*YHWH*' has been used from Chapter 2 of the Bible right up to the present verse, this is the moment that God first reveals and explains His name to mankind, **Exodus 6:3**. And the newly invented pictographic Hebrew alphabet would now capture the name in a way that expressed something of both its life and resurrection.

We have already seen, in *Volume 2: Jesus in the Beginning*, pages 46–51, how:

> **I, I Am: Exodus 3:12–15** firmly associates the name *YHWH* / יהוה with the verb 'to be' / *hayah* / הוא. It is a quirk of Hebrew grammar that it doesn't have a distinct way of uniquely marking the present tense, so the famous phrase 'I am who I am' is much broader in meaning. It is more like: 'I-was-am-and-will-be who I-was-am-and-will-be', which is perhaps why in **Revelation** God / Jesus says: 'I am the Alpha and Omega . . . who is and was and is to come . . . ', **Revelation 1:8**. The Ancient Greek translation of the Bible, the Septuagint, tries to convey this broader sense of 'I am' in this passage by using the emphatic phrase ἐγώ εἰμί / 'I, I am', a phrase picked up and used frequently by Jesus in the Gospels, **John 18:8**, though English versions often drop the first 'I'.

> The Resurrection: We also saw how the new pictographic letters told a story, creating not just words but painting hieroglyphs as well. While the name '*YHWH*' was spelt (right to left) צ𐤘𐤟, the glyphs read 'the-hand-see-it-the-nail-see-it', which is the sign of the resurrection asked for by Thomas who wanted to ' . . . see in his hands the imprint of the nails . . . ', **John 20:25**.

> And the Life: '*YHWH*' is spelt with only 'breath' letters (consonantal-vowels) because 'God is Spirit',

John 4:24 (in Hebrew 'spirit' and 'breath' are the same word *ruach* / רוח). While many Rabbis made a point of not speaking the name *YHWH* out loud, they also observed that every time someone breathed in and out they sounded out *YHWH*'s name: breath in 'ee-aa' / *Yah*, breath out 'oo-aa' / *Wah*. God's name was the sound of life. Now grammatically, *YHWH* approximates to the causative third person form of that verb 'to be', *hayah* / הוא, so it has been suggested that *YHWH* could mean 'He lives' or 'He causes to be'. I quite like 'He lives-life'.

The name *YHWH* adds up to Jesus' statement: 'I, I am the Resurrection and the Life', **John 11:25**.

First and Last Signs

Next, *YHWH* gives Moses two 'signs' which in their own way speak to how salvation will work in **Exodus** and how it works in Christ. The two signs represent two sides of salvation.

The first sign – Salvation

Moses throws down his staff and it becomes a serpent. Moses flees from it, **Exodus 4:2–5**. A rearing snake, called the 'Uraeus', was the symbol of Egypt's gods and of Royal authority, *the* things Moses had fled from 40 years before. On *YHWH*'s instruction, Moses grabs the snake by the tail and breaks its fear over him. Salvation starts by *YHWH* breaking the hold of the demonic over us. Egypt was what *YHWH* saved Israel from, but it was not what He saved them for . . .

The second sign – Sanctification

Moses' hand turns leprous before *YHWH* heals it. The Biblical word for leprosy, *tsara* / צרע, is much broader than its modern definition, covering all sorts of rotting or spoiling infections. Salvation redeems us from the debt against us *and* it sanctifies us, cleansing us from the rotting influence of sin on everything we do. Holiness is what we are saved for – 'you shall be to me a kingdom of priests, and a holy nation', **Exodus 19:6**.

The first half of **Exodus, chapters 1–19**, details 'Salvation' as *YHWH* leads the people out of Egypt. The second half, **chapters 20–40**, are about 'Sanctification' as *YHWH* gifts the people the means to get clean, from the ten commandments to the tabernacle.

All the plagues on Egypt are presented as a part of the first and last 'signs' . . .

It could be that if they neither believe you nor listen to the voice of the first sign, that they will believe the voice of the last sign. It will happen, if they will not believe even these two signs . . . then you shall take of the water of the river and pour it on the dry land . . . The water which you take out of the river will become blood on the dry land. **Exodus 4:8–9**

The word sign in these verses is made up of the first and last symbols of the Hebrew alphabet, a sacrificial bull, aleph-$\aleph$, and a cross, tav-$+$. That little word *AT* that we've seen time and again points us to the Crucifixion.

 History hinges on the Christophany of **Exodus 3–4**. It sets the framework for understanding salvation, declaring the whole story of **Exodus** as the complete sign of saving and sanctifying sacrifice. This is why I use the burning bush as the icon to mark appearances of 'the image of the invisible God', **Colossians 1:15**.

This is a good point to transfer some notes into your Bible

Part 3

Plagues & Passover

Tutimaos

J osephus calls the Pharaoh of the Exodus 'Tutimaos'. Tutimaos is first mentioned in a history of Egypt written in Greek by an Egyptian priest called **Manetho** in the third century BC. **Manetho** tells us, 'Tutimaos, in his reign . . . God smote us . . . '

The Exodus Pharoah of the **Traditional model** is Thutmose II. In the **Radical** model there is a Pharaoh Dudimose II 40 years after Moses' step-father Sobekhotep IV. Both 'Dudimose' and 'Thutmose' could be alternative Greek translations of 'Tutimaos', but 'Tutimaos' does not fit the Pharaoh of the **Standard** model, 'Ramesses', so well.

If **Josephus** and **Manetho** are correct, the Pharoah of *the Exodus* is either Dudimose II or Thutmose II.

The Passover Cup of Jesus

The response of Dudimose / Thutmose to Moses' message, 'Let my people go', is to increase the Israelites' forced labour, **Exodus 5:5–9**. As Moses complains to *YHWH* that His plan is not working, *YHWH* conveys a message through Moses to His people that is recited to this day by Jews and symbolised by Christians in Communion:

> Therefore tell the children of Israel, 'I am *YHWH*, and I will bring you out [**Sanctification**] from

> under the burdens of the Egyptians, and I will deliver you [**Deliverance**] out of their bondage, and I will redeem you [**Redemption**] with an outstretched arm, and with great judgments: and I will take you to me [**Restoration**] for a people, and I will be to you a God; and you shall know that I am *YHWH* your God . . . ' **Exodus 6:6–7**

The four **promises** and the quality of salvation which each exemplified were commemorated by sharing wine at the Passover meal, though the manner has varied over time; each diner's cup may have been filled four times, four cups may have been used or a single cup may have been shared four times. It is this shared cup that is referred to in **Psalm 116:13** as the 'Cup of Salvation', quite literally the 'Cup of Jesus'.

Jesus turned this shared cup into communion, drawing all its promises and qualities into His own sacrifice. Luke's Gospel shows Jesus using the 'Cup of Salvation' at least twice during the meal, see **Luke 22:17,20**. The Cross fulfilled spiritually the promises that *the Exodus* had achieved historically.

Christus Victor

Jesus' Cross is an eternal event that happened in history. It is a complex paradox without a perfect analogy, but as Christians have sought to understand it, formulating theories of atonement, it is clear that it has three dimensions:

- **God-ward – Satisfactional Model**: Something in God is satisfied, be that His honour or His justice.
- **Man-ward –Moral Model**: The Cross reveals, challenges and changes something in mankind's morality.
- **Sin / Devil-ward – The Victory of Christ**: The Cross defeats and humiliates the power that holds us by letting that power have its own way, only to fail on its own terms. Theologians give this model of the atonement the term, **Christus Victor**.

We will look at all three aspects of the Cross in *Volume 5: Jesus in the Wilderness*, but here we will focus on **Christus Victor**, the defeat of the power that binds us, because **Exodus** is very clear that the Plagues and the Passover were spiritual warfare.

> I will execute judgement against all the gods of Egypt . . . **Exodus 12:12**

David affirms the idea that *the Exodus* was a redemption *out from* the gods of Egypt: 'Your people whom you have redeemed for yourself *from Egypt's nations and its gods* . . . ', **2 Samuel 7:23**. (Note the phrase 'Egypt's nations': Egypt comprised at least two nations, Upper and Lower Egypt and was often a confederation of more mini-states, in a similar way to the United Kingdom, which is made up of four states and other territories.)

Furthermore, Jethro sees Egypt's gods as active in the plagues: 'Now I know that *YHWH* is greater than all gods because of the thing in which they dealt arrogantly He was above them', **Exodus 18:11**. The plagues were not sent arbitrarily by *YHWH*, they were the outworkings of the Egyptians' own theology and worship. *YHWH*'s victory was seen in the failure of Egypt's gods when given the freedom to be what they really were. They had freedom, but He was still in control.

YHWH gave Moses a 'first sign', to control and take hold of a snake that would devour the other snakes of Egyptian religion. The Uraeus, the serpent symbol of Egypt's authority, didn't just appear on Pharaoh's headdress, it appeared on the headdress of many of Egypt's most important gods. They all derived their meaning from 'the serpent of old, the Devil', **Revelation 12:9,20:2**, who the Egyptians knew by many names, including Apep (see below).

Victory Against All Gods

> He seized the dragon the ancient serpent who is devil . . . and tied him up . . . **Revelation 20:2**

We know the names of over 1400 ancient Egyptian deities, but there are thousands more we don't, so we can't say exclusively and exhaustively how each plague addressed each and every minor deity. However, there are clear connections between Egypt's pantheon and the disasters that befell them. The plagues are *theological*.

In an ancient Egyptian document, **Ipuwer's Admonitions**,

usually dated to the end of the thirteenth dynasty, the sage **Ipuwer** admonishes the reigning Pharoah by recalling disasters he himself has witnessed as the result of a previous Pharaoh not dealing with foreigners. **Ipuwer** even reports that, because of the calamities on Egypt, 'Behold, men have fallen into rebellion against the Uraeus', the rearing snake that was Pharaoh's spiritual authority.

Ipuwer's Admonitions has parallels with the Biblical plagues but is normally rejected as being corroboration for *the Exodus* for two reasons: the events seem too disastrous, and it is written too early for the **Standard model**.

But **Ipuwer's** testimony fits easily with the dates of *the Exodus* if we follow the **Radical model** and possibly even the **Traditional model**. **Ipuwer** helps to make the plagues *historical*, not just *theological.*

Interestingly all 10 plagues have also been shown to be the natural effects of just three causes, one biological, one environmental and one cultural (see below). Those who believe *the Exodus* was a fabricated story now have to explain how its ancient inventor came up with a run of events that makes perfect scientific sense in the twenty-first century. The Plagues are not just *theological* and *historical*, they are *scientific* too.

We will consider these three perspectives as we look for the prophetic (📖) and Christo-telic (📕) meaning of the plagues.

Plague 1: Water turns to blood and kills the fish

Jesus' first public 'sign' was turning water into wine, **John 2:1–11**. This sign was good news for the wedding guests, but bad news for the kingdom of darkness. The plagues on Egypt were triggered by a similar sign.

> The Bible: ' . . . you shall take of the water of the river, and pour it on the dry land. The water which you take out of the river will become blood on the dry land.' **Exodus 4:9**

> Ipuwer: 'See Egypt has fallen to the pouring of water, and he who poured water on the ground seizes the mighty in misery, *see the serpent has been taken from its hole* . . . ' **Admonitions**

> The Bible: 'Moses and Aaron did so . . . in the sight of Pharaoh, and in the sight of his servants; and all the waters that were in the river were turned to blood. The fish that were in the river died; and the river became foul, and the Egyptians couldn't drink water from the river; and the blood was throughout all the land of Egypt.' **Exodus 7:20–21**

> Ipuwer: 'The river is blood! As you drink of it you lose your humanity and thirst for water'. And later, 'That is our water! That is our happiness! What shall we do about it? All is ruin.' **Admonitions**

The Nile river was the life of Egypt. The Nile god *Hapi* was called the 'Father of Egypt' and was depicted with breasts and a pregnant belly to symbolise the life he brought.

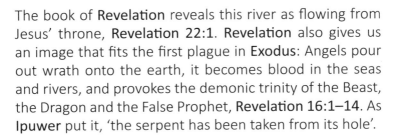

Jesus would one day stand up and declare: 'If anyone is thirsty, let them come to me and drink . . . as the Scripture said "from his belly shall flow rivers of living water"', **John 7:37–38**. Jesus is referring to the river seen by Ezekiel who prophesies: ' . . . there shall be a very great multitude of fish . . . everything shall live wherever the river comes', **Ezekiel 47:9**. Jesus kicks off His public ministry with the huge catch of fish, **Luke 5:7**.

The book of **Revelation** reveals this river as flowing from Jesus' throne, **Revelation 22:1**. **Revelation** also gives us an image that fits the first plague in **Exodus**: Angels pour out wrath onto the earth, it becomes blood in the seas and rivers, and provokes the demonic trinity of the Beast, the Dragon and the False Prophet, **Revelation 16:1–14**. As **Ipuwer** put it, 'the serpent has been taken from its hole'.

Hapi represents the demonic counterfeit of what Jesus was, is and will be. The fish in *Hapi's* river died as the water turned to 'blood', a theological sign which triggers a chain of natural or scientific phenomena.

The Red Nile

We know that the Nile can be turned red by the silt bought by the August inundation. But this was a blessing – it fertilised the land, fish didn't die, and water was still potable. But when the York River (Virginia, USA) turned red in the 1990s millions of fish did die where it flowed into Chesapeake Bay.

This red river was caused by a bloom of *Gymnodinium breve* algae. There are many red algae which can kill fish, they tend to bloom where fresh water rivers, rich with nutrients, mix with salt water. At least one type of algae, *Oscillatoria rubescens* (commonly known as 'Burgundy Blood'), can thrive in totally fresh water. In Egypt, the Israelites were located where the fresh water Nile flows into the salt water marshes of the Nile delta.

Egypt is hottest in September shortly after the annual inundation has bought in nutrient-laden red silt. Algal blooms require food and heat. The rich silt which feeds the algae would also feed tadpoles, before the algae killed the fish.

Plague 2: Frogs everywhere

In **Revelation**, the rivers and seas turning to blood causes ' . . . three unclean spirits, just like frogs' to come out of the Beast, Dragon and False Prophet, 'they are spirits of demons . . . which go forth . . . for the war of that great day of God, the Almighty', **Revelation 16:13**. In **Exodus**, *YHWH* continues to expose the gods of Egypt.

Frogs swarm in the Nile from September to October. Tadpoles develop more quickly in contaminated waters but will leave them as soon as they become frogs. The plague of frogs is the natural consequence of the dead fish and spoiled water of the first plague. The frogs forced out of the Nile looked for damp, wet and shady locations wherever they could find them.

> . . . Go in to Pharaoh, and tell him . . . 'I will plague all your borders with frogs: and the river shall swarm with frogs, which shall go up and come into your house, and into your bedroom, and on your bed . . . into your ovens, and into your kneading troughs . . . ' **Exodus 8:1–4**

Frogs were well thought of in Egypt. They were associated with birth and resurrection to the afterlife, because they emerge transformed out of the water. The frog goddess, *Heket*, was given the title 'She who hastens the birth' and her image was carried by women during pregnancy.

In the **Osiris myth**, *Heket* is associated with *Osiris'* resurrection, breathing life into a body for his posthumously conceived son *Horus*.

Heket's worship survived well into the Christian era. Medieval *Heket* amulets have been found containing the words of Jesus, 'I am the resurrection', alongside images of the Cross.

In the plague of frogs, we see *YHWH* dealing with a demonic parody of His own resurrected Son, the true resurrection and life who breathes His life into His new body the church, **John 20:22**.

When *Heket's* frogs died, there was no resurrection, 'they gathered them together in heaps, and the land stank', **Exodus 8:14**. Jesus' sacrifice was a sweet-smelling fragrance, **Ephesians 5:2**, that led to new life.

Plagues 3 and 4: Midges then Flies

The next two plagues are both bug-borne. First, small 'biting insects' / *ken* / כן (#H3654), gnats, midges or lice, are produced out of the 'dust of the earth'. Then larger 'swarming insects' / *arob* / ערב (#H6157), flies or even beetles descend onto the 'ground'. The Egyptian priests are unable to replicate these plagues.

> Stretch out your rod, and strike the dust of the earth, that it may become midges throughout all the land of Egypt. They did so . . . and there were midges on man, and on animal; all the dust of the earth became midges throughout all the land of Egypt. **Exodus 8:16–17**

The eventual death of Egypt's livestock (see Plague 5) implies that the 'biting insects' were *Culicoides* midges which transmit several deadly diseases and parasites.

In October to November infection spreads as midge numbers soar along the Nile because their natural predators, the frogs, are all dead. At the same time the piles of dead frogs accumulate, the perfect breeding ground for the subsequent plague of flies.

Midges

> Bible: 'The magicians tried with their enchantments to produce midges, but they couldn't'. **Exodus 8:18**

> Ipuwer: 'Spells are frustrated because they are remembered by men'. **Admonitions**

The plagues of midges surpass the power of *Thoth*, the god of Magic invoked by the priests.

And the midges had come up out of the 'dust of the earth'. The Egyptian god over the dust and earth was *Geb*, who had a role in judging the dead (those buried in his earth). *Geb* was called the 'father of snakes' and was depicted with a snake for his head.

Jesus, who will judge the living and the dead, **2 Timothy 4:1**, would one day crush the serpent's head, **Genesis 3:15**.

Flies

The plague of 'biting insects' is followed by one of 'swarming insects'. *Kepri* the god of creation, rebirth and the movement of the sun, was depicted with a fly or beetle's head (beetles were considered larger versions of flies in the ancient world).

Kepri's name means 'come into being'. The ancient world believed that insects simply 'came into being' in dirt, dung or dead bodies. Aristotle gave the idea of 'spontaneous generation' a philosophical foundation in the fourth century BC, so the idea persisted in common thought right up to the nineteenth century. John's Gospel affirms that, 'all things were made by him [Jesus] . . . without him nothing was made that was made', **John 1:3**.

The plague of flies only affected the Egyptians. **Exodus** calls this division between the Egyptians and Israelites a 'sign', **Exodus 8:23**. The word used is that little marker word *AT*, the aleph-א and tav-ת depicted in Israel's early alphabet as ✝𝒴. The sign of the 'crucified sacrifice' was the difference between those who would be saved and those that would not.

I've considered the third and fourth plagues together, because midges and flies are both representative of the part of creation represented by *Kepri* god of bugs and beetles. Throughout Jesus' ministry, He was accused of doing miracles by the power of *Beelzebub / Beelzebul*.

Beelzebub was a Philistine god, not an Egyptian one. But his name meant the 'Lord of the flies / flying things'. *Zebub / זבוב* (#H2070) is a generic word covering all flying insects from midges to beetles. Later Aramaic slurred the last part of his name so that it sounded like *zebel* which meant 'dung', perhaps because flies seem to spontaneously generate in manure. To the Jews, '*Beelzebub*' became a derogatory name for Satan, the adversary, the power actually being fought in the third and fourth plagues of **Exodus**.

Plague 5: Sickness and death of livestock

The Bible: '. . . see, the hand of *YHWH* is on your livestock which are in the field, on the horses, on the donkeys, on the camels, on the herds, and on the flocks with a very grievous pestilence . . . *YHWH* did that thing on the next day; and all the livestock of Egypt died, but of the livestock of the children of Israel, not one died.' **Exodus 9:1–6**

Ipuwer: 'Indeed, all animals, their hearts weep; cattle moan because of the state of the land'. **Admonitions**

There are two viruses that will kill all the livestock listed above, African horse sickness and bluetongue. Both are transmitted by the *Culicoides* midges of the third plague.

There are a lot of minor Egyptian deities linked to livestock, but *Hathor*, one of the most important and popular goddesses often appeared as a cow or with the head of a cow. *Hathor's* son, *Hapi-ankhu*, eventually became the Apis-bull, the flesh and blood earthly representative of the creator god *Ptah*. Perhaps anticipating the life of Jesus, the Apis-bull would be ritually sacrificed, mummified and then re-incarnated in a new-born calf, ready to re-cycle the parody or prophecy all over again.

Hathor herself was the goddess of love and protection, one of her roles was welcoming the dead into the afterlife. *Hathor's* role is a poor imitation of Jesus', as Paul writes:

> For I am persuaded, that neither death, nor life
> . . . nor any other created thing, will be able to
> separate us from the love of God, which is in
> Christ Jesus our Lord. **Romans 8:38–39**

The loss of large numbers of livestock showed the failure of *Hathor's* protection, though we don't know specifically what happened to her son, the Apis-bull.

And the failure of Egypt's various livestock gods was not over yet. The timeline for the plagues is now into December.

Plague 6: Boils on Cattle and People

> The Bible: 'They took ashes of the furnace, and
> stood before Pharaoh; and Moses sprinkled it up
> toward the sky; and it became a boil breaking out
> with boils on man and on animal.' **Exodus 9:10**

> Ipuwer: 'Plague is throughout the land. Blood is
> everywhere'. **Admonitions**

Flies can spread various illnesses that produce boils and welts on the skin. Perhaps these sores were evidence of glanders which is caused by the *Burkholderia pseudomallei* bacterium carried by flies.

Whatever the cause, its impact on Egyptian culture was profound, because the magician-priests all became ceremonially unclean at a stroke, **Exodus 9:11**. The plague of boils caused the functional collapse of the entire Egyptian religious system, leaving the population with no formal means to please and petition their gods.

In particular the plague of boils would have been an indictment on *Sekhmet* the goddess of healing and the bringer of plagues, and of the failure of *Isis* the 'compassionate' goddess of healing and magic. Both these gods had key roles in the protection of Egypt and the Pharoah.

The healing of 'lepers' was one of Jesus' signature miracles, **Luke 7:22**, and we saw earlier how Biblical leprosy covered all sorts of skin peeling and lesions, including boils and blisters. Jesus healed what *Sekhmet* could not prevent.

Interestingly at the time of *the Exodus* (**Radical, Traditional** or **Standard** dating) there was a cult in Egypt that revered and prayed for healing to an historic polymath healer, Imhotep. 'Imhotep' means 'the one who comes in peace'. His cult lasted well into the second century AD and I can't help but wonder if there were those who recognised in the Gospel what they had been searching for in Imhotep's cult, what they 'worshiped in ignorance' they now had declared to them, **Acts 17:23**.

The first six plagues have run over a period of nearly five months. They are all connected by a scientific chain of cause and effect that was initiated by a biological event, the blooming of red algae. What follows comes out of the blue . . . quite literally.

The next three plagues are also connected, this time by a natural meteorological event.

Plague 7: Hail and Fire on Fields, Flax and Barley

> The Bible: '*YHWH* sent thunder and hail, and the fire travelled on the ground . . . hail struck through all the land of Egypt . . . both man and animal; and the hail struck every herb . . . every tree . . . The *flax and the barley are ruined*, the flax was in the ear the barley in bloom, but the wheat and the rye were not smashed; for they were not yet grown up'. **Exodus 9:23,25,31**

> Ipuwer: 'What was seen yesterday has perished, the land is left to its tiredness by [the time for] the cutting of *flax* . . . ' **Admonitions**

Flax is in the ear almost ready to harvest, and barley is flowering in late January. This is when the seventh plague struck.

The serpent-headed goddess *Renenūtet*, the 'lady of the fields', was responsible for the harvest. Her son, *Nepri* was 'god of the risen grain'. Both failed in their duties.

While every crop was damaged, the total loss of flax and the barley had wide and instant ramifications.

Flax fibres make linen from which *Nepri's* wife *Tayt*, goddess of linen and weaving, fashioned clothes for the gods. But everybody wore linen of varying quality, it was even used to clothe the dead. Linen was used for everything from fishing to filling teeth and processing flax was a major industry.

Barley produced both bread and beer, the currency with which working Egyptians were both paid and made offerings to their gods. The beer was low in alcohol and was a clean way of replacing water lost through the day whilst providing vital sugars, complex carbohydrates, minerals, amino acids and vitamins.

Egyptians even entered the afterlife equipped with a prayer that asked for 'bread and beer, beef and fowl, ointment and clothing, everything good and pure to the soul . . . ' (inscribed on multiple funerary objects, coffins, stelae, paintings, jewellery and amulets etc). Flax and barley sustained and clothed the Egyptians from cradle to grave.

 Jesus once observed that the Gentiles were anxious for 'what shall we eat?', 'what shall we drink?' and 'with what shall we clothe ourselves?' but that our heavenly Father knows our needs before we ask, **Matthew 7:28–32**. The Egyptians looked to *Renenūtet*, *Nepri* and *Tayt* for these basics, but they failed.

This damage to the fabric of Egyptian life was inflicted both by hailstones and by 'fire that travelled on the ground'. Many modern translations obscure the detail that the 'fire' / *esh* / אש (#H784) 'travelled' / *halak* / הלך (#H1980) on the ground, opting for the easier to understand 'lightning flashing onto the ground'. But the Hebrew description is scientifically more informative.

The Bible doesn't mention rain. This is significant because most wildfires across the whole world are caused by 'dry storms'. In hot wilderness regions, the rain produced by a storm in the high atmosphere never reaches the ground, it evaporates as it meets the hot air rising from the dust below. The evaporation creates a heavy cold layer that pushes down on the rising hot air, making ground conditions windy but dry. When lightning occurs the vegetation ignites easily and the fires 'travel' across the ground fanned by warm winds.

> The Bible: 'there was hail, and fire mingled with the hail.' **Exodus 9:24**

> Ipuwer: 'Indeed, gates, columns . . . are burnt up . . . Behold, the fire has gone up on high, and its burning goes forth against the enemies of the land.' **Admonitions**

The cold layer in this otherwise warm atmosphere can also create large hailstones. The cold layer grows colder until falling rain freezes instead of evaporating. The frozen rain descends into the rising hot air which pushes it back up through the cold layer where it collects more ice. The hailstone will cycle up and down through the cold layer collecting ice until it is heavy enough to fall through the updrafts. This process can produce huge hailstones.

To the Egyptians, these hailstones and fire represented the failure of *Nut*, the sky goddess, whose arched blue body held the outside chaos away from the inhabited earth. *Nut* would sometimes take the form of a cow and other times a sycamore tree, so it is interesting to note that both her symbols were struck by the hail.

The Bible: 'the hail *struck* . . . all that was in the field, both man and animal; and the hail struck every herb of the field, and *broke* every tree of the field.' **Exodus 9:25**

Ipuwer: 'Indeed, trees are felled and branches are stripped off.' **Admonitions**

 It was as though the Egyptian Pantheon had become a diabolical house divided against itself, something Jesus hints at, **Luke 11:15–20**. And the infighting isn't over yet.

 Plague 8: Locusts devour the surviving grain

The Bible: 'Moses stretched out his rod . . . and when it was morning, *the east wind* brought the locusts . . . and they ate every herb of the land, and all the fruit of the trees which the hail had left. There remained nothing green . . . through all the land of Egypt.' **Exodus 10:12–13,15**

Ipuwer: 'Behold, grain has perished on every side'. **Ipuwer** describes the full loss of taxable produce caused by the disaster he has seen, 'The entire palace is without its revenues. To it belong wheat and barley, geese and fish . . . ' **Admonitions**

The locusts are blown in from the eastern desert by storm winds. *Senehem* was a locust-headed minor deity. *Seth*, god of deserts, storms and violence was a major player. He was a fickle trickster at constant war with *Horus* (who protected the fertile land) but daily fighting back the serpent-god of chaos, *Apep* (later known as *Apophis*). *Apep* is pertinent to understanding the plague of darkness. But for this eighth plague, it is *Senehem*, the locust god, who causes the damage.

Locusts are simply hormone-pumped versions of common grasshoppers. When conditions push the grasshoppers together, a rush of serotonin transforms them into fast breeding, constantly eating, monster hoppers. The wild fires and winds that preceded the hail would have created the conditions that encourage locust swarming. The entire harvest is consumed by them.

In contrast, at the same time of year, early Spring, about 1500 years later, **John 6:4**, Jesus will sit people down in a place with a lot of grass, **John 6:10**, and feed 5000 men plus women and children. Afterwards Jesus' disciples '. . . filled twelve baskets with broken pieces from the five barley loaves, which were left over by those who had eaten', **John 6:13**.

Back in Egypt we read: '. . . *YHWH* shifted the wind to a *very strong west wind* which took up the locusts and drove them into the Sea', **Exodus 10:19**.

Plague 9: Darkness

The Bible: '*YHWH* said to Moses, "Stretch out your hand toward the sky, that there may be darkness over the land of Egypt, even darkness which may be felt." Moses stretched out his hand

. . . and there was thick darkness in all the land of Egypt for *three days*.' **Exodus 10:21,22**

Ipuwer: 'The land is without light . . .' **Admonitions**

Strong winds from the west of Egypt can pick up sand from the Sahara and form a wall or a blanket of dust and sand called a 'haboob'. Haboobs often happen as thunderstorm systems collapse. There is a famous description of the effects of one of these dust storms by a Victorian engineer.

. . . I saw approaching from the South West . . . immense brown mountains high in the air. So rapid was the passage of this extraordinary phenomenon that in a few minutes we were in actual pitchy darkness. At first there was no wind and the peculiar calm gave an oppressive character to the event. We were in 'a darkness that might be felt' . . . This lasted for upwards of twenty minutes: then rapidly passed away, and the sun shone as before, but we had felt the darkness that Moses had inflicted upon the Egyptians.
Major R H Brown, Inspector General of Irrigation, Royal Engineers, 1899

Dust-induced darkness typically lasts for just a few hours. As hours turned into days fear must have given way to apocalyptic panic.

Egyptian mythology encoded an elaborate theology of the battle between *Ra*, the sun-god of light, and *Apep / Apophis*, the evil snake-god of chaos, who encircles the world. Every day *Apep* waited just below the horizon to destroy light and truth as *Ra* descended into the underworld.

It was fickle *Seth's* job to protect *Ra* from *Apep*. *Seth* was aided by priests and ordinary worshippers who performed rituals and spells prescribed in **The Books of Overthrowing Apep** every single night. But the priesthood had collapsed with the plague of boils and there was no bread or beer for normal offerings.

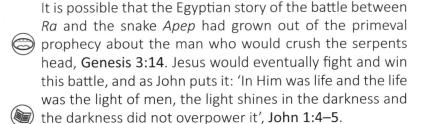

It is possible that the Egyptian story of the battle between *Ra* and the snake *Apep* had grown out of the primeval prophecy about the man who would crush the serpents head, **Genesis 3:14**. Jesus would eventually fight and win this battle, and as John puts it: 'In Him was life and the life was the light of men, the light shines in the darkness and the darkness did not overpower it', **John 1:4–5**.

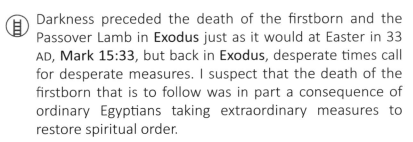

Darkness preceded the death of the firstborn and the Passover Lamb in **Exodus** just as it would at Easter in 33 AD, **Mark 15:33**, but back in **Exodus**, desperate times call for desperate measures. I suspect that the death of the firstborn that is to follow was in part a consequence of ordinary Egyptians taking extraordinary measures to restore spiritual order.

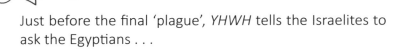 Plague 10: Passover and death of the firstborn

Just before the final 'plague', *YHWH* tells the Israelites to ask the Egyptians . . .

The Bible: '. . . for articles of silver and articles of gold and clothing. And *YHWH* had given the people favour . . . so they [Egyptians] let them [Israelites] have their request. So they plundered the Egyptians.' **Exodus 12:35–36**

Ipuwer: 'Gold and lapis lazuli, silver and malachite, carnelian and bronze . . . are fastened on the neck of female slaves.' **Admonitions**

That night, '*YHWH* struck all the firstborn in the land of Egypt, from the firstborn of Pharaoh who sat on his throne to the firstborn of the captive who was in the dungeon; and all the firstborn of livestock . . . there was a great cry in Egypt because there was no home where there was not someone dead', **Exodus 12:29**.

Over the course of his warning, **Ipuwer** states: 'there is groaning throughout the land, mingled with lamentations'. **Ipuwer** contrasts how 'the children of princes are dashed against the walls' and even 'the prison is ruined', **Admonitions**.

Ipuwer implies that this mass death is a combination of sickness and personal violence: 'Hearts . . . are violent, pestilence is throughout the land, blood is everywhere, death is not lacking . . . ', **Admonitions**. While the Bible doesn't unpack how death swept through the Egyptian firstborn, it is not hard to imagine a combination of sickness alongside desperate ritual killings and retributive violence.

Ancient Egypt didn't practice human sacrifice as part of worship, but both inscriptions and excavated remains show that that ritual killings were an expectation when a religious sanctuary or holy rite had been transgressed or an evil needed to be fought against (eg Senusret I's inscription at Monthu's Temple in Tod; and ritual remains from the fortress at Mirgissa).

Whatever the mechanism behind this loss of the firstborn, **Ipuwer** was to observe: 'Men are few, and he who places his brother in the ground is everywhere . . . '

 At Passover, Israel sacrificed a lamb that had lived as part of the family, to protect their firstborn and free them for a new way of life. Easter fulfilled Passover, 'God so loved the world He gave His only-born Son, that whoever believes in Him should not perish, but have everlasting life!', **John 3:16**.

 The Gospels are conscious about the way *YHWH*'s actions in the past acted as prophetic models or 'types' reworked and retold in Jesus' life (see **Matthew 2:15**). But the moments they acknowledge are not the whole story, and with hindsight we can see Jesus' story reflected in the whole flow of the Plagues to Passover, as the table opposite illustrates.

YHWH's words and actions create shapes and ripples which run through all salvation history!

Plagues to Passover	Jesus' First to Last Miracles
The Exodus escape starts with Moses pouring out water *that becomes* blood. The water of Egypt becomes undrinkable . . . Exodus 4:9	For Jesus' first public miracle, He instructs the wedding servants to pour out water that becomes wine. *The new wine is better than what went before.* John 2:1–11
. . . and the fish die. Exodus 7:20–21	Jesus starts his Galilean ministry with a miraculous catch of fish. Mark 1:16, Luke 5:1–11
Frogs *go out into the places where people live.* Exodus 8:1–4	The only New Testament reference to frogs is in Revelation, where frog-like demons go out into the world.
	Jesus' first action after the miracle of the fish is to deliver a man in the Capernaum synagogue, who has an evil spirit. Mark 1:23–27
Midges and flies spread disease throughout the land. Exodus 8:16–17,24	News about Jesus goes out everywhere. People start coming to Jesus who heals them, then Jesus goes *'throughout all Galilee'* to heal and deliver. Mark 1:28,33–34,39
People (including the Egyptian priests) *are* covered in sores and welts, *the priests are no longer able to minister.* Exodus 9:11	Jesus heals a man of leprosy and sends him to be declared clean by the Priests. Mark 1:40–45

The plagues enter a new phase when the sky turns against the Egyptians with fire, hail stones and strong winds. **Exodus 9:23–25**	Jesus is asleep in a *storm*, He wakes, rebukes the storm and it obeys His command. **Mark 4:37–41**
The storm is followed up by a numberless army of locusts. **Exodus 10:13**	After calming the storm, Jesus delivers a man of a *'Legion'* of demons. **Mark 5:7–17**
The harvest is destroyed. **Exodus 10:15**	'The harvest is plentiful but the labourers are few' so Jesus sends out the 12. **Matthew 9:37–10:1, Mark 6:7**
Nothing green is left to eat. **Exodus 10:15**	Huge crowds gather on the green grass, Jesus feeds them. **Mark 6:35–44**
Darkness precedes the Prototype Passover. **Exodus 10:22**	Darkness precedes the Fulfilled Passover, **Mark 15:33**.
The Prototype Passover: Death of the firstborn and the death of the Passover lamb.	The Fulfilled Passover: Death of The Firstborn who is the lamb of God.

Timeline of the Plagues of Egypt

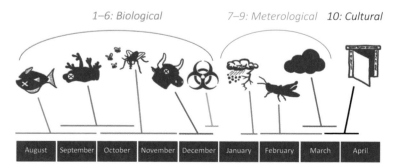

1–6: Biological   7–9: Meterological   10: Cultural

| August | September | October | November | December | January | February | March | April |

⑨ The Sign of the First Passover

The Passover is the defining ritual of Judaism. A vast number of customs and meanings have been attached to it over the years, but the word itself contains meaning.

The Hebrew word for 'Passover' is *peshach* / פסח (#H6453) and is first used in **Exodus 12:11**. The same three letters, פסח, are used two verses later, but here they are given a different **Strong's** number, #H6452, and are translated 'pass over' because the simple meaning of the word 'Passover' is 'hop', 'skip' or 'jump', see **1 Kings 18:21,26**. But the same three letters have an older meaning.

The first-century Targum, **Onkelos** (35–120 AD), reminded Jews who now spoke Aramaic that *peshach* / פסח is related to 'mercy'. This matches modern research which traces the word back to Akkadian, the Semitic language that preceded Hebrew, where it meant to 'placate'.

'Passover' does not imply an ignoring of sin, it is not an 'over-looking' nod and a wink, it is mercy achieved by the placating or settling of a debt. A simple lamb, however perfect and innocent, would never be enough, but it was a parable of what was to come.

And there is more in the word 'passover' too. Over time the rabbis noticed a coded message in its three letters: Pey-פ, Samakh-ס and Heth-ח.

Pey-פ is the seventeenth letter of the Hebrew alphabet. As a word, *pey* / פה (#H6310) is usually translated as 'mouth', but it can be translated as 'speech', 'words', 'message' or 'command'. Its oldest pictographic form was a mouth or pursed lips, ⌣.

Samakh-ס is the fifteenth letter of the Hebrew alphabet. Its symbolism is complex and developed. As a word, *samakh* / סמך (#H5564) means 'to lean against / into'. It is also used for the laying-on-of-hands, so *samakh* was important to both blessings and sacrifices in the book of **Leviticus**, and it is the word used for God's support and help in **Psalm 3:5**.

The shape of the letter Samakh-ס adds to its meaning. The current glyph 'ס' is thought to represent a shield, and the previous pictogram represented a thorn bush, ⍑, hedges of which were used by ancient Israel as protection, see **Psalm 89:40**.

Finally the letter Heth-ח was associated with both sin because it sounded like a word for 'sin', *heta*; and with grace because Heth-ח represented the number '8' which was linked to grace. The current glyph for the letter, 'ח', can be seen as both a barrier (sin) and as a doorway-through-a-wall (grace).

So the pictograms used by Moses' generation to write the word 'Passover' conveyed:

> 'A message(⌣) about protection(⍑) from sin(⊞)'
> or 'a command(פ) to lean into(ס) grace(ח)' !

Passover is pictographically  : a message-of-protecting-grace.

There is more on the meanings of these letters and the whole Hebrew alphabet in *Volume 1: Jesus in the Old Testament*.

In **Exodus 13**, *YHWH* commands the Israelites to bind the 'sign' of the Passover on their heads and hands. Taking this command literally led to the wearing of amulets / phylacteries / tefillin by Jewish men. We will explore the meaning of the verses in this amulet in *Volume 5: Jesus in the Wilderness*.

But had the Hebrews been a little more literal, they would have bound the word 'sign' to their heads and hands. And we noted earlier, they would have written the word 'sign' with an aleph-𐤀, a wav-𐤅, and a tav-✝, which were a sacrifice, a nail and a cross.

They would have remembered Passover, a message-of-protecting-grace with a sign showing 'a divine-sacrifice-fixed-to-a-cross'.

 This is a good point to transfer some notes into your Bible

Part 4

The Exodus
& The Road to Sinai

Flight from Egypt

Exodus **14–19** tells the climax of *the Great Escape*! The flight from Egypt; the crossing of the Red Sea; and end of the Egyptian army; the provision of food in the wilderness; Israel's first battle with their long-term nemesis; and finally, the people's arrival at Sinai.

Just as we saw typological parallels between the events from Plagues to Passover (see table on pages **63–64**), so the events of **Exodus 14–19** pre-empt chapters **3–8** of **John's Gospel**. The parallels are thematic and symbolic rather than literal and precise, history is repeated in spirit. (Note: a less detailed version of this table appeared in *Volume 1: Jesus in the Old Testament*.)

Exodus Event	Gospel Event
The people pass through the Red Sea / Sea of Reeds. Exodus 14:1–15	Huge crowds come to Jesus and His disciples to be baptised. John 3:22, 4:1–3
Travelling through Shur, the Israelites come to Marah where *YHWH* makes the bitter water sweet. Exodus 15:22–25	Travelling through Samaria Jesus comes to Jacob's Well, where Jesus promises those who drink from Him will never thirst. John 4:4–42
YHWH promises freedom from sickness and leads the people to the Elim Oasis where there is abundant food. Exodus 15:26	Jesus continues through Galilee, healing people as He goes until the 'Feast' in Jerusalem where He heals the man at the pool of Bethesda. John 5:1–15

People accuse Moses of leading them to their death. Exodus 16:1–3	People accuse Jesus of being a false witness, Jesus likens His rejection to Moses' rejection. John 5:16–47 (see verses 46,47)
Promise of Manna. Exodus 16:4–7	Feeding 5000 and the Bread of Life Sermon. John 6:1–40
Provision of Manna and quail meat in a context of complaint. Exodus 16:8–36	Complaint in the context of Jesus providing bread and 'flesh' to eat. John 6:41–71 (see verses 48–54)
Relocation to Rephidim. Exodus 17:1	Relocation to Judea. John 7:1–10 (see also Matthew 19:1, Mark 10:1, Luke 9:51)
Quarrelling with Moses. Exodus 17:2	Grumbling among the crowds. John 7:11–36
People are thirsty. Exodus 17:3–4	Is anyone thirsty. John 7:37
Water is provided from the rock. Exodus 17:5–6	Living water is promised from the believer's innermost being. John 7:38–39
Opposition to Moses and conflict with the Amalekites. Exodus 17:7–16	Opposition from the authorities. John 7:40–53
Moses acting as Judge. Exodus 18:1–27	Jesus acting as Judge. John 8:1–11
YHWH is seen in the cloud. Exodus 19:1–25	Jesus reveals Himself as God. John 8:12–59

We will explore Israel's journey through Sinai more thoroughly in the next book in this series, *Volume 5: Jesus in the Wilderness*, but it all starts at the Red Sea.

The Red Sea and the Walls of the Ruler

The Hebrew Bible calls the 'Red Sea', *yam-suf* / ים-סוף which means the 'Reed Sea' or 'Sea of Reeds'. We get the name 'Red Sea' from the ancient Greek version of the Old Testament, the Septuagint, and from **Josephus**. This is confusing because reeds can't grow in salt water like the modern 'Red Sea'.

But reeds can grow in fenland, areas where freshwater lakes drain into sea, and modern archaeology has shown that in ancient Egypt a chain of inland waterways followed and filled the geological fault line from just below the Mediterranean to the top of the Gulf of Suez. Seismic activity and the Suez Canal have shifted and reshaped these lakes, but three of them survived right into the twenty-first century: the Bitter Lakes in the South, Lake Timsah in the middle and the Ballah Lakes in the North.

During the 1990s, archaeologists **Amihai Sneh** and **Tuvia Weissbrod** of the Geological Survey of Israel uncovered an ancient system of canals (each over 70 metres wide) which joined these lakes together to form a great defensive barrier. Ancient Egyptian hieroglyphs refer to such a barrier, calling it 'The Walls of the Ruler', it had forts, bridges and crocodiles, and it was full of reeds.

'The Walls of the Ruler' created a reed-filled extension to the Red Sea. It was why the Israelites had to cross a body of water at all. Today the Suez Canal stops you walking directly into Sinai from lower Egypt – in Moses' day, the Walls of the Ruler were no less an obstacle.

After the Israelites reached Etham on the western edge of the wilderness they were trapped, **Exodus 14:3**. Then *YHWH* appears as columns of cloud / smoke and of fire and leads them back northwards (towards what would become Ballah lakes), **Exodus 14:2**. Moses will eventually name these columns of fire and smoke 'Jesus', as we will see below.

The Crossing Point

Exodus 14 includes three place names or descriptions that can be identified with some confidence.

> *YHWH* spoke to Moses . . . 'turn back and camp facing Pi-hahiroth (that is between Migdol and the sea), you shall camp facing Baal-zephon on the opposite side and by the sea. For Pharoah will say . . . "they are wandering aimlessly in the land [ie Egypt], the wilderness has shut them in."' **Exodus 14:1–3**

First, Pi-hahiroth is made up of *Pi* / פי / 'mouth or edge of', *ha* / ה / 'the', and *hiroth* / חרת which is the plural form of a root-word that means 'something cut / bored out', such as a trench or a canal. Hebrew often uses a plural to convey big size so Pi-hahiroth is 'the mouth of the canals' or 'the mouth of the big canal'.

Second, this 'big canal' lies between 'the sea' and 'Migdol', a tower (the Hebrew word *Migdal* / מגדל / tower became a loan word *Migdol* in Egyptian).

Third, in the opposite direction from the canal and tower is a place with a Canaanite name, 'Baal-zephon'. Baal Zephon is the name of a Canaanite god worshiped by traders settled in the Egyptian town of Tahpanes. A papyrus held in the British Museum (**papyrus Anastasi III**) refers to a body of water in this region as 'the Waters of Baal'. So, Baal-zephon is thought to be a shrine outside Tahpanes and close by the inland sea.

This single body of water, the 'Waters of Baal', was known by the Egyptians as 'Pa Tjufy' which simply means 'The Reeds'. 'The Reeds' was the northern end of the reed filled basin that ran down to the Gulf of Suez, the Red Sea, and became known to the Ancient Hebrews as 'yam-suf' the 'Reed Sea'.

Over millenia, the 'Reed Sea' crossed by Moses became the Ballah lakes, which in turn became the Ballah Bypass on the original Suez Canal before it was eventually swallowed up by the New Suez Canal in 2015.

Despite being the northern-most point of the 'Walls of the Ruler', the Israelites couldn't simply walk around the top of 'The Reeds' because the ancient canal works extended eastward into northern Sinai. This forced everyone travelling into and out of Egypt through a narrow strip of land on the Mediterranean Coast. This passage, called the Horus Road or the Way of Horus, was fortified with eleven fortress towers (*Migdal*).

The location of the 'Migdol' referred to in **Exodus 14:2** has been identified (by Prof Kitchener, Prof Hoffmeier and others) as the third tower along the Way of Horus, the 'Migdol of Menmaatre / Seti' referred to in various ancient Egyptian texts. Today it lies unexcavated under a commercial fruit farm a little north east of what was once the Ballah Lakes.

The Israelites camped just 10 miles south of the Mediterranean where the ancient inland sea curved towards the east. Ahead of them were the Egyptian border fortresses and forces, behind them was the Egyptian army. Taking the Biblical detail seriously shifts the story from fabulous to factual, the same is true of what comes next.

Jesus Leads the People out of Egypt

> Moses said to the people, 'Don't be afraid, stand still and see *YHWH*'s Jesus (salvation), the thing He will do for you today: So, the Egyptians you see today, you shall never see again. *YHWH* will fight for you, and you shall be still . . . and God's Messenger who had been going ahead of the Israelite camp moved and went behind them . . . He came between the camp of Egypt and the camp of Israel, there was a cloud with darkness which gave light at night so the one [ie Egyptians] didn't come near the other [ie Israelites].' **Exodus 14:13–14,19–20**

Moses tells the people to stand still and watch *YHWH*'s Jesus / salvation, which in Hebrew is written:

את ישועת יהוה

Jesus' name, ישוע, is prefixed with the aleph-tav, את / *AT*, the first and last sacrifice, and suffixed with a tav-ת which was written with a cross, ✝ at the time of *the Exodus*. This extra ✝ simply makes 'Jesus' belong to *YHWH*; it is similar to adding 's in English to get *YHWH*'s Jesus.

 Without realising it, Moses gives a name to God's Messenger (who is seen in the columns of smoke and fire) and to His activity. He is 'Jesus' and He leads the people through the waters to salvation.

Knowing where the Reed Sea was crossed gives us a slightly different perspective on the miracle of parting the waters. This phenomenon has been observed in modern times precisely as described in **Exodus** at Lake Menzala, just 15 miles north and west of the northern strip of the Ballah Lakes.

In 1882, British Soldier and statistician **General Alexander Tulloch** witnessed and recorded the event:

> An easterly gale came up very rapidly . . . Next morning . . . to my astonishment, I noticed that Lake Menzala on the west side of the canal(Suez) had disappeared beyond the horizon in that direction and the Arabs were walking on the mud where the day before boats had floated . . .

In the hours that followed the waters returned. Now science refers to this type of event, where strong wind acting over a long period moves water from one location and piles it up somewhere else, as 'wind set-down'.

This is what the Bible describes (and note the reference to the 'wall'):

> . . . And *YHWH* caused the sea to go back by a strong east wind all the night, and made the sea dry, and the waters were divided. The children of Israel went into the midst of the sea on the exposed ground, and the waters were a wall to them on their right hand, and on their left.
> Exodus 14:21–22

General Tulloch's observations led Dr Carl Drews of the US National Center for Atmospheric Research (NCAR) to devise a computer model of this phenomena on Lake Menzala. His results, published in 2010, concluded that an east wind of 63 miles per hour blowing for half a day would open up a land bridge 2.5 miles long by 3 miles wide.

Now Lake Menzala is larger than the Reed Sea was, but it is a part of the same system of inland seas, all of which could be affected by this rare but real phenomenon. Some may feel uncomfortable accepting a natural explanation for a miracle, but nature itself is God's first and greatest miracle. It is my experience that Jesus regularly acts supernaturally by natural means.

And the fact that the Bible describes the Reed Sea crossing in language that fits the technical requirements of 'wind set-down' is hard to explain if it had never actually happened. In this respect it is rather like Jesus' sweating blood before His death. Luke's account is the first description in history of hematidrosis or blood sweat. Its causes and processes in times of extreme stress are now well understood, but a first-century author would not and could not have invented it if it hadn't actually been witnessed.

In *the Great Escape*, as in the Crucifixion, God has told a story rich in mythological meaning but in the language of political, social and natural history.

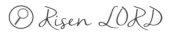 Risen *LORD*

Moses had told the people to watch *YHWH*'s Jesus / Salvation and, having experienced it, the Israelites commemorated it in a song. 'The Song of the Sea', **Exodus 15:2–18**, forms the oldest piece of liturgy in the Bible. It finishes with the first ever reference to the reign of *YHWH*, the Kingdom of God. As we read on it seems that the song was initiated by Miriam, Moses' sister. The longer version (sung by Moses and all the Israelites) would have taken time to come together and was added to as the people built up history in the wilderness. (Notice it refers to Edom, Moab and the Canaanites, none of whom have yet been encountered).

Miriam is called 'The Prophetess' when she sings the first line of *the first corporate worship song*, 'Sing to *YHWH*, for He is highly exalted'. But those last two words are actually the same Hebrew word, *gaah* / גאה (#H1342) which figuratively means 'glorious' or 'majestic', but more literally means to 'rise up' or be 'risen'.

An amazing point of parallel symbolism occurs between **Exodus 14 and 15**. Messenger–*YHWH* identified as 'Jesus' / Salvation leads the people through the sea, a Biblical symbol of death, and a lady called Miriam declares: 'Sing to *YHWH*, for He is risen risen'. This declaration is picked up by the main leader, Moses, and the rest of the people.

On the first Easter, Jesus went into death and rose again, making a way through for us. Then a woman called Miriam – Mary in our English Bibles – was the first to meet the risen Jesus, a fact she declares to Peter and the other disciples!

Now when Moses picks up Miriam's opening lines, he adds 'Jesus' to it: '*Yah*, my strength and song, has become my Jesus (salvation) and this one is my God and I will praise Him . . . *YHWH* man-who-does-battle *YHWH* is His name', **Exodus 15:2–3**.

Moses declares that '*Yah* . . . my Jesus is my God!' Before going further to describe *YHWH* as a 'man' / *aish* / איש (#H376). *YHWH* is a 'man of battling' / איש מלחמה, which modern translations turn into 'warrior', avoiding any confusion in calling God a 'man'. However, we have seen in previous books how the use of divine plurals hints at the Trinity and so the use of *aish* surrounded by two '*YHWHs*' hints at structure in the three parts of *YHWH*'s plurality. It puts something human-like in the very centre; furthermore the word *aish* (#H376) is a contracted form of the word *anosh* / אנוש (#H605) which means 'mortal'. 'Adam' also meant man, but *aish* emphasised a man who would die. Adam's grandson was called *anosh* because He was born into a dying world, we know him as 'Enosh'.

 With hindsight we can see that (by the Spirit) Moses' praise revealed a part of God made vulnerable in the battle for mankind's salvation. Because '*YHWH* mortal man-who-does battle *YHWH*' is His name!

Exodus is about to give us a model of God's salvation as a man-who-does-battle, in Joshua, who fights the Amalekites and whose name is the older spelling of 'Jesus'.

 This is a good point to transfer some notes into your Bible

Marah, First Stop on the Road to Sinai

After crossing the Reed Sea, the Israelites headed south into the desert and three days later they came to a place where the waters were bitter. Three days' travel (65 miles) south of the place we identified as Pi-hahiroth we find a region called Bir el-Mura or 'the bitter well' to this day because the water is brackish. Here, *YHWH* shows Moses a tree which can be used to make the water drinkable and *YHWH* declares Himself as *YHWH*–Rapha or '*YHWH* who heals you' before taking them on to Elim where there is a well for every tribe, **Exodus 15:22–27**.

The image is a wonderful type of the Cross. The Hebrew word used here for the 'tree' which made the water clean is *etz* / עֵץ (#H6086). It can also be used for wooden structures of execution (see **Esther 2:23** and **5:14**) like the Cross.

Now if Moses burnt the tree before adding it to the salt-laced water, it would be the oldest recording of a technique still used by nomads today. Charcoal from the red acacia / acacia seyel tree purifies salty water. Moses' divinely inspired action worked as history *and* provides a typological myth-story that points to Jesus.

Just nine miles south of modern Bir el-Mura is 'Elim', an oasis now called Ayun Musa / 'the springs of Moses'. Here an underground aquifer cleans the salty water and supports scores of date palms just as **Exodus** describes.

Manna and Meat

Around May time, a month after moving on from Egypt, the Israelites set out into the wilderness again. They start complaining straight away, so *YHWH* 'gave them bread from Heaven to eat', **Exodus 16:4**. The crowds quote this same verse at Jesus the day after He miraculously feeds 5000 in the wilderness, **John 6:31**. They see Jesus as a free meal and want more to eat. Instead Jesus reveals: 'I am the bread of life', **John 6:35**, 'so the Jews were grumbling . . . because He said, "I am the bread that came down out of Heaven"', **John 6:41**. As a type, manna is a model of both what Jesus is and what He does for us.

Moses' response to the people's complaining prophetically anticipates Jesus, referring to God in both the second and third person and foreseeing that He would be seen: 'You will see the glory of *YHWH* (visible God), for He (invisible God) hears your grumbling against *YHWH* (visible God), and what are *we* that you grumble against *us*?', **Exodus 16:7**.

 The people see the 'glory of *YHWH*' that evening in the cloud as God provides quail meat then in the morning there is manna on the ground, **Exodus 16:10–14**. The crowds quote this passage at Jesus that day after He has miraculously provided fish meat and bread, but puzzlingly He tells them that '**no-one has** seen the Father, except the one who is from God', **John 6:46**. It has always been God the Son who reveals God the Father, **John 1:18**. Jesus was the glory the people saw in the cloud which became quail meat to eat and the glory they saw on the ground, the bread from Heaven.

Thousands upon thousands of quails migrate to Europe from both Africa and Arabia beginning in late April and through May each year. Bedouin still catch them as they land, exhausted, to feed. Manna is well researched in the Sinai Peninsula too. An insect, the *Coccus manniparus*, ingests the sweet sap of various trees and excretes honeydew onto the ground and flakes of a lichen, *Lenora esculenta*, will sometimes fall like rain. A mix of these two phenomena match the full biblical description of manna; it was both flaky, seed-like and sweet, **Exodus 16:31** and it could be baked or boiled, **Exodus 16:23**. It is still eaten today.

The natural sources of manna and quail don't diminish their miracle. Every year water gets turned into wine by natural processes. Jesus' first miracle was more about timing and quantity than product and process. Manna and quail were about grace and provision.

Now interestingly, **Numbers 33:10–12** tells us the route which the Israelites took, so we know the manna and quail happened at or near a place called 'Dophkah'. This location is found in Egyptian records and is called 'Du Mofka'. It is the plateau surrounding the mines of Serabit el-Khadim where archaeologists first unearthed Hebrew words written in Egyptian hieroglyphs.

In 2018, a scholar in ancient Hebraic texts, **Michael Bar-Ron**, translated a piece of graffiti found on a wall in one of those mines. In the middle it reads:

> 'Who is for the Father in regards to your Manna?'
> **A Notice About Manna and Uprooted Oppression**
> **at Serabit el-Khadim, Rabbi Michael S. Bar-Ron**

The message is signed by someone called **Arba**. The Israelites were given detailed instructions on how to properly honour the gift of manna, **Exodus 16:15–36**. This ancient bit of graffiti seems to be encouraging that respect.

So it is tantalising to think that the 'Father' referred to in this text is perhaps Moses. 'Father' is too intimate a name for *YHWH* at this point. It is Jesus who popularises the name 'Father' for God, because Transcendent-Creator-God can only be known intimately as 'Father' when He is known through the experience of His Son who reveals Him!

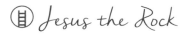 Jesus the Rock

The Israelites continue eastwards coming to Rephidim, where the people continue to quarrel with Moses and 'test' *YHWH*, **Exodus 17:2**. This time a lack of water prompts the challenge 'Is *YHWH* among us or not?', **Exodus 17:7**. Moses answers the complaint by striking a rock which starts running with water. The rock becomes a sign that *YHWH* <u>is</u> among the people, a sign fulfilled by Jesus as 'Immanuel, God with us', **Matthew 1:23**. So Paul tells us: 'For they drank of a spiritual rock that followed them, and the rock was Christ', **1 Corinthians 10:4**.

While at Rephidim, now called Massah ('Test') and Meribah ('Quarrel'), *YHWH* gives the people another picture of His presence among them in the Bible's first reference to Joshua, the victorious leader whose name becomes *Yshua* in later Hebrew and 'Jesus' in Greek.

The Amalekites come out to fight the Israelites, so Moses selects and sends Joshua against them.

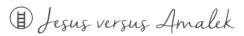 Jesus versus Amalek

Amalek was a grandson of Esau. Esau was renamed 'Edom' / אדום (#H123) because he sold his birthright for some 'red stuff' / *adm* / אדם (#H122). This is spelt with the same letters as 'Adam' / 'Man' / אדם (#H120 and #H121), see **Genesis 25:29–30**. Notice how 'man', 'Adam', 'red stuff' and 'Edom' form consecutive Strong's numbers, H120-123 – they are all part of the same root word.

Now Jacob had the 'red stuff', because Jacob 'stewed stew' / ויזד יעקב נזיד. The word doubled up in this phrase is זיד / *zid* (#H2102), which means both to 'boil' / 'stew' and to be 'proud' / 'presumptuous'.

Jacob 'stirred-up proud-stuff' and proud Esau bought it becoming Edom the 'proud-adam'. His descendants were the 'Edomites', spelt אדמי, which simply means 'of Adam'.

Typologically, the Edomites stood as a model of the human pride that fought against God's Kingdom. Historically the Edomites were Israel's first enemy represented by the Amalekites here in **Exodus**, and they were still fighting the Israelites at the end of the Old Testament in **Malachi 1:4**. Finally, Herod the Great and his family were Edomites too. Three generations of Herods persecuted Jesus, as a child, as a man, **Acts 4:27**, and finally in His church, **Acts 12:1**.

Jesus' final victory over 'prideful humanity' is fore-shadowed by this first victory of His name-sake Joshua.

Edom is represented by the people of his grandson Amalek, a name that probably derives from *malak* / מלק (#H4454) meaning to 'crack' or 'shatter'. It is used in **Leviticus 1:15** for wringing the necks of birds. Saul's future failure to deal with the Amalekites, **1 Samuel 15:1–11**, leads ultimately to his death, and it is an Amalekite that deals him the death blow, **2 Samuel 1:7–10**.

But, in this first typological battle, Moses sends Joshua, promising to preside over the battle in prayer. While Moses' hands are raised, Joshua prevails; when they are lowered Amalek has the advantage. In the end Aaron and Hur hold Moses' arms up and Joshua wins, **Exodus 17:9–13**.

The incident paints a profound image. Moses represents the Law and the Old Covenant but, standing on the hillside with his arms outstretched, Moses shows us the Cross. Jesus' final victory took place under the Law, it was that Law that showed us what it meant. If we only see rules in the Old Testament we are in trouble, but the Law can be a tutor that leads us to Christ and justification by faith, **Galatians 3:24**.

In Jesus we can finally 'put away . . . the old-humanity' proud Adam, 'and put on the new', **Ephesians 4:22–24**.

 This is a good point to transfer some notes into your Bible

Conclusion

Joshua's victory over the old humanity is a good place to end this volume. Moses memorialises the win with an altar to '*YHWH* my banner' and declares: '*YHWH* has sworn; *YHWH* will have war against Amalek from generation to generation', **Exodus 17:16**.

The Cross happened under the law, its victory is immutable and our Salvation is complete, but Christ in us continues to war against the old Adam as we are transformed from glory to glory. Having taken the Israelites out of slavery, *YHWH* spends the next 30 years taking slavery out of the people. The journey into holiness and promise is the subject of *Volume 5: Jesus in the Wilderness*.

In **Exodus 18** Moses' authority is being delegated into the people, with leaders being set over tens, hundreds and thousands of people. Moses' father in-law, Jethro a pagan high priest, sums up the first half of the book of **Exodus** with a statement that reflects his own conversion:

> Now I know that *YHWH* is greater than **all the gods**, in their presumptuous words He was above them. **Exodus 18:11**

Jethro offers sacrifices to *YHWH*.

In **Exodus 19**, the Israelites arrive at Sinai and it is the 'third month'. *YHWH* appears to Moses and gives him the Law. The event is commemorated by the Festival of

Reaping or Weeks, **Exodus 23:16** or **34:22**, the Day of First Fruits, **Numbers 28:26** and later called *Shavuot*. It is better known to us as Pentecost.

It is interesting to note that on the day that the gift of 'The Law' was given, 3000 people died for their sin, **Exodus 32:28**, but at Pentecost when the Holy Spirit was given, 3000 people were saved! First fruits of a spiritual harvest.

YHWH writes theology in history and Scripture together. Mythology becomes the language of theology and the stories, retold to children and examined by scholars, get into our hearts in a way that changes individuals and whole nations alike.

The Great Escape is done but the book of **Exodus** is just halfway through. The events of the second half of **Exodus** are also recorded in **Leviticus**, **Numbers** and **Deuteronomy** and will be covered by the next book in this series:

5
Jesus in the Wilderness
Signs & Wanders

Leviticus – Deuteronomy

$\mathcal{S}ummary$ The big contribution of **Exodus** to our understanding of Jesus is in *Types* and *Teaching* – the book illustrates and illuminates the theology of Salvation in words and images:

Salvation itself is a type of Jesus: it's the noun ישוע that becomes His name. **Exodus** represents salvation through a story of Divine intervention to release the enslaved by a substitute death, then by baptism through water and a journey towards a future promise.

The story becomes a teaching parable, one that gives us words and ideas expanded and explained by Jesus and the Gospels.

Now, while **Exodus** lacks verbal prophecy it still prophesies. Jesus' ministry and miracles recapitulate events from Plagues to Passover, and from the Red Sea to Sinai.

And the Burning Bush (one of three visible appearances of God in **Exodus**) gives us the icon we use for the pre-incarnation Christophanies . . .

during that appearance we see the Divinity of Messenger-YHWH.

Looking a little deeper we find the declaration 'He has risen, risen' as a celebration of Salvation, the words first sung by 'Miriam' (Mary in Greek) and a group of women.

Jesus' direct family doesn't really appear in **Exodus**; there's passing mention of two generations, Amminabad and Nahshon, as well as a missing generation. We'll look at them all together in *Volume 6: Jesus in War & Peace*. But the whole book of **Exodus** is about Jesus' wider family – the promises given through Abraham, Isaac and Jacob would have been lost but for *the Great Escape*.

If this book has inspired you to re-read this amazing adventure story with fresh eyes, it has done its job. If it has challenged you to see how *God is writing Jesus' testimony in your story,* even better.

Feel free to be in touch at jesuscentred.org and join the discussion!

Jesus in the Old Testament Series (proposed plan)

Jesus in the Old
Testament: OUT
An introduction   NOW
Genesis – Malachi
978-0-9933445-1-0

Jesus in the Beginning:
Creation & Primeval History
Genesis 1 – 12   OUT
978-0-9933445-5-8 NOW

Jesus in the Fathers:
Patriarchs & Promises
Genesis 12 – 50   OUT
978-0-9933445-7-2   NOW

Jesus in the Great Escape:
*Out of Egypt I have called
my Son*   THIS
Exodus   BOOK!
978-1-912947003

Jesus in the Wilderness:
Signs and Wanders
Leviticus – Deuteronomy
OUT 2019

Jesus in War and Peace:
*The Age of Heroes and
Heroines*
Joshua – Ruth

Jesus in the United Nation:
*Under an anointed Prophet,
Priest and King*
1 &2 Samuel – 1 Kings

Jesus in Division and
Defeat:
*Prophetic Purpose in a
Broken People*
2 Kings – 1 & 2 Chronicles

Jesus in Words of
Wisdom:
For Life, Love and Loss
Job – Song of Songs

Jesus in Worship and OUT
Wonder: NOW
*Melody, Mystery and the
Messiah* Psalms
978-0-9933445-9-6

Jesus in the Major
Prophets:
*Incarnation, Crucifixion,
Resurrection and Ascension*
Isaiah – Daniel

Jesus in the Minor
Prophets:
Revealing the Plans of God
Hosea – Malachi

Jesus in Exile and
Return:
Creating a Space for Grace
Ezra – Esther + input from
the prophets

Jesus in the Silent Years:
*Providence in the Wait for
The Messiah*
End of the Old Testament
to start of the Gospels